PLANTS
AS
PETS

PLANTS AS PETS

by Robert P. Bauman

With illustrations by
Patricia Jones Bauman

DODD, MEAD & COMPANY
NEW YORK

1 2 3 4 5 6 7 8 9 10

Library of Congress Cataloging in Publication Data

Bauman, Robert P.
Plants as pets.

1. House plants. 2. Indoor gardening. I. Title.
SB419.B22   635.9'65   81-9874
ISBN 0-396-08021-9   AACR2
ISBN 0-396-08028-6 (pbk.)

APPRECIATION

This book would not have happened—history will judge whether it should have!—without Pat Hass, who inspired me to write it and whose help and work made it possible.

*This book is dedicated to my mother,
who planted the seeds that developed
my interest in the wonderful world of plants,
and to my family—Patsy, John, and
Elizabeth—who have encouraged this
interest and helped care for our plant pets.*

Contents

PLANTS
AS
PETS

1
Planting the Idea

As far back as I can remember, pets were part of my life. Dogs, cats, canaries, fish, and even a duck wandered in and out of our house in Cleveland, Ohio, as I grew up, and their companionship was a joy. Some of our pets were beautiful, some propagated a lot—and the year I spent teaching my dog tricks I learned that pets can be an interesting hobby, too.

The first plants I met were vegetables. Tomatoes, carrots, and cucumbers thrived in my mother's garden behind our house. Though they weren't boon companions—unless nourishing our bodies is counted as nourishing our spirits—I learned from them as I hoed and picked that plants living in the natural world can be very resilient.

We had houseplants, too. My mother always kept them in the living room, kitchen, and bedrooms. Mine suffered through periods of drought when I forgot to water them and flood when I tried to make it up to them. But they survived, and sometime in that period I discovered how companionable plants can be. I became so attached to those plants that I took them with me to college.

When I went into the Air Force and after that got my first job, I was too busy to think about pets and plants until I was married and bought a house. Then we got our first dog and cat, and I began to accumulate plants again. Right away I ran into trouble.

My job required frequent travel, and sometimes I was away for long periods of time. There was hardly time to even talk to my plants—let alone take care of them. Still, I wanted to keep them, and I wanted them to stay healthy, so I read plant books and talked to friends. They said things like this:

"Plants are delicate. Plants are fragile. They need special care and attention or they die."

"You need a green thumb."

"They may look pretty in the shop, but once they're in the house they stop blooming."

"It takes hours to maintain your plants."

"Plants? Prima donnas."

Very frustrating information, and besides it didn't ring true. I did not remember my mother's vegetables and houseplants being that delicate, and my college days had proved that plants could survive under trying circumstances. I wanted to enjoy my plants, not worry about them. Other people were having the most extraordinary "luck" with plants, or so it seemed, despite the fact that they put their plants in the "wrong places," watered them at the "wrong times," and treated them very casually.

These people seemed to be taking their plants out

of their normal environment and putting them in places where plants don't usually grow. But the plants were flourishing! What was going on? I wasn't sure, but these people certainly were in control of their plants, not the other way around. I also thought: Could this control evolve further, into a kind of training?

Would it be possible to train my plants to live the way I wanted them to, to adapt them to *my* schedule? My wife and I had already done this, in a way, with our dog and cat, when we fed them after our dinner hour and walked them at the times we wanted to. And we enjoyed them more. Would it work with my plants?

I didn't have much choice. With such a tight schedule I had to do something drastic if I was going to have healthy plants, or keep plants at all. And my plants were definitely fun to have. What I had to do was to eliminate the worry, not the plants.

Very gradually I began to introduce my plants into the erratic conditions of my life. I observed how the plants adjusted, and if I was going too fast, I backed off a little. To my surprise, they responded and began to thrive. And, more surprising, they seemed to welcome the limited attention and companionship I was able to provide. Why? Because responding means surviving, and plants want to survive.

Suddenly I realized I was treating my plants the way I treated my dog and cat. My plants were my pets too! But what terrific pets—lovely, companionable creatures who would not chew my socks or wet the living room rug. Better yet, they were not noisy, did not have fleas, and generally speaking, did not snarl at my guests even when the dregs of a drink were poured into their homes or a cigarette was squished out on their heads.

It wasn't a difficult transition to make in my mind and as you read on and we go through the adapting process together, you think about it too—isn't a plant one of the very best pets you could have?

The first thing you do is relax. Don't brood about the whys and wherefores and if you're doing the right thing; just think in terms of helping your plant pet adapt to you and your household.

Next, memorize the following:

Worry is out.
Plants want to survive.

You'll become more and more aware of the steely quality, the toughness, and instinct for survival that a plant represents as you provide the simple things your plant needs like air, water, food, and light, and you sit back and watch your plant become accustomed to your schedule. It won't take long, once your plant is trained and relating to you and your requirements, for you to notice that your plant is attached to you as well. (This attachment is similar to that of a dog's, but without all the drooling.)

Eventually, you can train almost all kinds of plants, but since we're just beginning, you can improve your chances of success by picking the right plant.

2
Selecting Your Plant

The next time you find yourself in the supermarket's plant section, about to grab a gardenia or geranium to brighten the table for a dinner party, STOP—and take a good hard look at what's in those plastic pots you're dumping willy-nilly into the cart. Those plants are about to become members of your household and you shouldn't run to the store to "pick up a few," not unless you want the results of a friend of mine. She has to buy new plants for every dinner party because they always die.

"I pick my plants for the way they look," she says, "and I don't ask the shop how long they'll last—they just have to make it through the party. Then I forget about them and when they begin to wilt, I throw them out."

There are better ways to choose your plants. Remember when you thought about getting a dog or cat? Didn't you read a few books, find out about the

Gardenia

breeds you were interested in, maybe ask friends? Or did you walk in to the pet shop, point to the Great Danes and say, "I'll take two of those." Once back in your efficiency apartment did you wonder why neither you or the dogs seemed to be having much fun?

Not all dogs are right for all people. If you're not crazy about vacuuming, you're probably not going to want a St. Bernard, a collie, or a sheep dog. If you want a watchdog, you probably will be unhappy with a Chihuahua. It's the same with plants. They, too, should be chosen with care.

How can you find out what kind of plant pet should be in your future? First, glance at the back of this book and you'll see a list of suggested plant pets. You'll be amazed to know that there are two hundred families of plants—and some families, like orchids, have 35,000 species!

Next, ask your friends for suggestions, and snoop around flower shops. When Willie Sutton was asked, "Why do you rob banks?" he answered, "Well, that's where the money is." If you want to find a pet, go where they are—plant shops, shows, nurseries, and botanical gardens. There are plant pets for everybody, and with so many to choose from you will not be limited to the same old cockers and retrievers.

After you have an idea of what you like, it's time to ask yourself the following very important question:

What do I want from my plant pet?

We know it's not protection—who ever heard of an attack plant? But people do want plants for all kinds of reasons, such as decoration, companionship, or as a lifelong, rewarding hobby.

Spider plant

Maybe you're looking for a status plant, a drop-dead arrangement of orchids that will impress your friends, or a grove of palm trees in your living room. Or, like some people, you want a long-lived plant. This is an unusual request, but not impossible to fill. There are many Methuselahs in the plant family—ancient oak, six-hundred-year-old pine trees, and dwarf plants like the bonzai that can live four hundred years in a small container. In fact, many ordinary houseplants can grow to be fifty years old. They might even live longer than you! (You can bequeath them to relatives and friends in lieu of stocks and money.)

Do you want a magnificent, multiplying, multitudinous plant? Then you should choose a spreading plant and just keep dividing and repotting. You'll have an unlimited supply for the price of one.

Maybe you don't have any special wishes or needs. You just like plants and want to own one. That's fine. But you still need to think about what you want from a plant, and it might help to consider the following points:

1. *What are your house conditions like?* Take a look at your plant pet's potential pad—your home. The size pet you pick will usually be determined by the space you have to share with that pet.

Do you live in a house? Apartment? Trailer? If you live in an old mansion, is it cold and drafty? Is your home sunny? Do you have a closed-in porch with a southern exposure? Do you have a basement? Plants love basements.

If your plant will be exposed to children, you may

want to consider something out of reach, perhaps a hanging pot, unless your child is a budding Tarzan!

"Hold it," you say, "I have a one-room apartment. It's cold in the winter and blistering in the summer. My only window faces a brick wall and the air is stifling. Can I still qualify as a plant pet owner?"

Emphatically, yes. Where you survive, so will your plant, but you do need to increase the odds of survival by picking a plant that will roughly fit into your conditions.

Suppose you travel a lot and you're out of town and you remember your plant has not had a drop of water for several days. You won't be able to drop everything and rush home. So, eliminate the problem in advance by getting a plant that can survive without water for longer periods of time. The plant will adapt ahead of crisis times because it has already become accustomed to your schedule.

2. *How much time and effort do you want to spend on your plant? A lot? Some? Very little?*

If you don't want to spend much time with your pet, or aren't able to, then you might enjoy the slower growing, more compact plants, because they are less work.

Small pot plants, hanging pot plants, hardy foliage plants fall into this category.

Fast-growing plants need pruning to stay contained, although they needn't scare you. Pruning is fun. After all, you're not trimming an orchard, just your pet to keep it in the shape you want.

And as you become confident and relaxed about

your plants, a strange thing will happen. You'll find you'll want to spend more time with them, maybe even produce a new type and give it your family name. But more on that later. Right now here are some plant groups to simplify things:

I. *Easily Grown Hanging Pot Plants*
   This is a beginner's special. You can't fail with any of these and they are attractive plants.
   1. Spider plants
   2. Hoya plant
   3. Swedish ivy
   4. Starlight or flame violet

II. *Small Pot Plants*
   Little plants that are slow growing or can easily be controlled by pruning. Attractive foliage and rewarding blooms. Very easy to grow.
   1. Beefsteak begonia
   2. Jade plant
   3. Bynura or velvet plant
   4. Christmas cactus

III. *Large Pot Plants*
   These plants are attractive and interesting, and you won't need a "green thumb" here either, just a little extra effort for a few of them.
   1. Citrus
   2. Hibiscus
   3. Gardenia

IV. Hardy Foliage Plants

Known for their attractive green leaves rather than flowers. Will grow under almost any conditions. They will survive well with very little light and can take neglect with great ease.
1. Corn plant
2. Fig plant or ficas
3. Radiator plant, or peperomia

V. A Final Twosome

Possibly the most rewarding plants on the entire list. Very easy to grow, believe it or not, and relatively inexpensive. If you want blooms, nothing surpasses the orchid. Individual blooms last weeks to months, and plants can produce twenty-five to fifty blooms each. Their reputation for fragility is unfounded; they deserve a place in everyone's house and are ideal as pets.
1. Orchids—magnificent blooms
2. Bromeliads—brilliant foliage

But, you say, suppose I *have* no choice. Suppose the doorbell has rung, and someone has walked in with a gift plant, or I was in the hospital and people sent me get-well plants that I've brought home. I've bought this book because I'm wondering, can I handle those plants? Or to put it the right way, will those plants fit me? Again, emphatically yes.

If you like the plant—and if you don't, quickly give it to a friend who does—you can fit that plant into *your* life, even if it's not a plant you would have

Corn plant

chosen, or not the ideal plant for your conditions. Your new plant will adapt. I'll say it once more: owning and raising a plant pet can be simple and pleasant, not a complicated, scientific experiment.

Okay. Now you're ready to choose a plant and put it in that shopping cart, or graciously receive one as a gift. Then say hello to your beautiful new pet plant and welcome it into your home.

3
Bringing Your Plant Home

Congratulations! You are the owner of a plant pet. Perhaps you've even given it a name. Something strong-sounding to discourage wilting. Rocky. Now, how do you decide where in your home Rocky is going to live?

Rocky will live and thrive where it is convenient for you. Your rubber plant may prefer the bathroom, but if you have to climb around it every time you brush your teeth, that rubber plant is in the wrong place. You are going to teach Rocky how to live in the place you want, to be part of your household in the area you choose.

So where *are* you going to put him? Remember that before you brought Rocky home, he lived in a nursery, but before that his ancestors thrived in the wild. This applies whether Rocky is a common houseplant, Swedish ivy, or an exotic orchid. In the wild, Rocky's forebears were left alone, to grow or to die. Somehow they survived changes in weather, temperature, insect attacks, bird bombardments, and animals nibbling away at their foliage. They developed very strong constitutions.

With that thought firmly fixed in your head, go over the basics. You have a windowsill, living-room corner, coffee table, hook in your dining room window, or family room. Plop your pet down where he looks pretty, where it's easy, where you want him to be for the moment. Then accept this important suggestion, which you won't find in pamphlets or books and won't hear about from plant store owners or friends. I call it: Having Living Quarters for your plant.

Don't worry, you won't have to set up the equivalent of a botanical garden in your home, nor am I suggesting you add even a small greenhouse. What I am saying is that you can put Rocky anywhere you want him, even if it goes counter to plant care instructions, because you have fixed another place that you think of, in your head, as Rocky's Living Quarters—where you will feed him, water him, groom him, doctor him, train him, or even breed him. This is for Rocky's protection and also for yours.

How for you? Well, you may love your dog, cat, or bird, but there are times when you tell the dog to go to his bed, the cat to get off your chair, and the bird to shut up. Or, you move his cage into a back room. You may even throw a cloth over the goldfish's bowl just so you won't have to see him for a while either.

It's all right to feel this way every now and then

because you've provided those pets with a space where they can be secure and rest, away from the main part of the house. Your dog has a house, your fish may even have a little castle in his bowl. This space is important to your pets, too—a place to go where the family is not.

It's just as important for Rocky to have Living Quarters. This is his real home. It's easier for you because you have a separate area with all the things you need to provide for him: water, potting soil, pots, fertilizer, and so forth. It's better for him because you can fix conditions that are more suitable than in other parts of your house by adding artificial lights and controlling humidity and temperatures. If you want to have several plants, they can all stay in the Living Quarters in peace without your worrying about their overall appearance, or even, on rushed days, having to see them. Gathered together, your plants help create their own environment, their jungle, if you will, and they will be very content. You can even increase your plant family and grow more than you ever could in your living room.

But for the moment, when Rocky is new, in bloom, or when you want his companionship or decoration, put him anywhere you like. Just remember that anywhere may be a bit dry or dark, and after a time he'll need a change. He may need pruning or repotting, he may have finished blooming, or he may just not look well. That's when you scoot him to his Living Quarters with its better conditions and attend to his needs with ease.

So now you have two places for Rocky—his regular or showplace and his kennel, or Living Quarters. You know where his showplace is—where do you put his kennel?

You can use a basement, garage, bathroom, corner of your kitchen, bay window, or whatever, and the area should allow winter nighttime temperatures between 60 and 65 degrees averaging 10 degrees less than average summer nighttime temperatures. Many plants can grow at lower or higher temperatures, but this suggested range will allow the greatest number of plant types to be grown. In addition:

1. There should be an easy place to add artificial light.
2. You'll need a faucet, ideally with hot and cold water. Plants prefer room-temperature water.
3. The space should be away from the heavy-traffic areas of the house so you don't have to worry about keeping it neat all the time.

A basement, if you have one, is an ideal spot for Living Quarters, especially if it has an unfinished area with a concrete or dirt floor. Your plants will enjoy the humidity. If your basement is below ground, the climate will be perfect for your plant—usually seventy to seventy-five in summer and sixty in winter.

Even a greenhouse or closed-in porch is not as good as a basement for Living Quarters. In the winter greenhouses and porches lose heat through the glass and need oil, propane, or electrical heat to keep your plants warm at night. In the summer they get too hot.

If your basement is small and the Living Quarters area is next to the furnace, it can get a little on the warm side during the winter. Most plants can take this warmth, but if you want to encourage growth you'll need a temperature change for them from day to night. Just leave a window open—the furnace is supplying heat up to the rest of the house and a little cold air in the basement will not affect the thermostat. But remember, I am talking about *best growth*. If you are satisfied with your plant growing somewhat below that criteria and it is too much trouble to bother with opening and closing the window—forget it. Your plant will survive.

No basement, try the garage.

If you are in an area where there are few freezing winter days, you can put a little electric heater in the garage for your plants; you'll have to turn it on only during those occasional frigid days each year, and that will take care of the climate requirements. A garage, like a basement, will have a concrete floor, faucet nearby, workbench, light fixture outlets. All you need is a corner of the garage for Living Quarters. In summer you'll welcome working in the comparative cool.

No basement, no garage, try the kitchen.

Frequently the kitchen has great humidity. Often it has spare space. Put some fluorescent lights under

Peperomia or radiator plant

a cabinet and grow your pets under that. Your kitchen is a plus as Living Quarters because water is immediately available.

Are you kidding? I have barely enough space in my kitchen for my pots and pans.

Kitchen too small? Then perhaps your bathroom. Water is available; you can grow plants on a shelf over the tub and when you water them they will drain right into the tub. Or take a shower. If it is a spare bathroom, you can close it off and not worry about the mess. Bathrooms usually have good light; if not, install a fluorescent one. By opening and closing the windows a crack you can control the temperature and humidity without affecting the rest of the house.

Living Quarters can be a spacious basement or garage, a nook in a kitchen, a corner of the bathroom, or even a few shelves over the washing machine. As long as there's light, water, food, and air it doesn't matter to the plant where you set it up.

Living Quarters for your plants is probably the most important concept in this book. This is the place you will keep most of your plants, where you can create ideal conditions, and take care of your plants the way you want to. The idea may sound strange at first, but it will make a big difference to your plants, and once you get used to it, you'll never give it up.

So, find a place in your house for Living Quarters. Believe me, it's worth it.

4
Furnishing Your Plant Pet's Living Quarters

Don't worry, I'm not going to tell you that curtains and a chaise are a must for your plant's psyche. But, just as a dog or cat requires a semblance of a bed, a dish for water and food, your plant requires a resting place as well. This "bed" can be a bench, a table, a bay window; just as long as you are able to feed and water your plant in his bed and there is a source of light and air (with reasonable humidity).

Building Your Plant Bed

My favorite plant bed is a bench with a slatted seat, about three feet high (this means less bending for you). The space between slats allows the water to drain freely so the roots won't rot. If your basement floor is dirt or concrete, just let the water drip through to the floor—as it dries you will be creating ideal humidity conditions. If you have a finished floor, put a tray under the bench. The space between the slats provides for air circulation as well as drainage. Go a little further and make the bench waterproof by painting it with a polyurethane finish.

Wire mesh makes an excellent bench top. The holes should be about one inch or less and the mesh should be nailed to a wooden frame that can be supported by wood or steel legs.

Build your plant bed bench to correlate with your light source. For example, if you have an eight-foot-long bench, 2½ to three-feet wide, your light fixture could be eight feet long and hang two to three feet above the bench. For further details, see the section on lighting.

Generally, twenty-four to thirty-six inches is a good width if your bench is still going to be covered by the light flow. Here are my suggestions for your plant bed:

1. Make your bench thirty to thirty-six inches high—a good working height.
2. Build a frame, using two-inch- by one-inch-thick eight-foot-long boards for the length of the top frame and twenty-four- to thirty-six-inch boards for the width.
3. For the bench top use wood slats one inch by two inches and eight feet long. The slats should be nailed down ¼" to ½" apart. Heavy gauge steel wire mesh can be used for the top instead of slats. Wire mesh does require a wire cutter, but perhaps the dealer from whom you obtain the mesh will cut it to size.

4. For the legs use two-inch by two-inch boards, thirty inches long, and attach the legs by L-shaped, four-inch by six-inch steel support braces, screwed to the legs and to the top of the frame.
5. In addition to the four corner legs, place a leg on each side and in the middle, to help support the plants' weight across the eight-foot bench top.
6. The wooden bench top and the legs should be coated with a clear, waterproof, polyurethane finish.

Cost: Lumber, L-steel supports, screws, and polyurethane finish should cost substantially less than buying a bench, assuming you can buy one to fit your needs.

Time: It will take around eight or ten hours to make the first bench but as your plant collection grows you'll be able to turn out your plant pets' beds in about five or six hours.

Note: When you use a small area, a kitchen or a bathroom, you will use a tray instead of a bench; the smaller the area, the smaller the tray. Your light source should be the governing factor for the size of the tray. Several times I have had metal-working or hot-air heating firms construct a tray to my specifications. Just remember to ask for a two-to-three-inch-high rim or side. Put pebbles or stones in the bottom of the tray and set your plant and pot on top to avoid direct contact with water. As this water evaporates you will be creating humidity for your plant's Living Quarters.

Lighting the Living Quarters

This is a subject that usually fills the new plant pet owner with dread. Mention lighting requirements for your pet plants and someone will say, "That's too complicated for me." But it doesn't have to be. Lighting, contrary to what you may have read, is not a magical talent reserved for those with a background in engineering.

You already know quite a bit about light. You know that humans and animals, birds and fish need light for energy/activity and darkness for rest. Common sense tells you that a change in the amount of light a plant receives can influence its growth and flowering patterns. And, of course, the intensity of light and the amount the plant can stand varies by specie. As with pets and humans, some can "take" the sun for longer periods than others.

Here's how the process works:

1. Plants use carbon dioxide (CO_2) and oxygen to produce their own food; they consume the food in order to grow, a process called respiration (see the illustration on page 28).
2. Sunlight or artificial light provides energy for the plant to make food—CO_2 from the air and water from the plant.
3. The combination of light, CO_2, and water pro-

1. Leggy growth

2. Normal growth

3. Bunched growth

Adequacy of light: 1. too little light; 2. proper balance of light; 3. too much light

duces organic materials, especially sugars, and this process is called photosynthesis.

Photosynthesis works better during the day when the temperatures are higher and the light is brighter. At night, as the plants consume the sugars, growth takes place. The illustration on page 29 will give you an idea of the cycle.

So when we talk about providing your plant pets with lighting it is not for cosmetic reasons. But what kind of light are we talking about?

Bright light is especially important for flowering, and books can tell you exactly the requirements of the plants you own. A typical plant book will indicate light requirement ranging from shade to full sun. (See the list in Appendix IV.) What I can tell you is that most plants have greater flexibility than this list would suggest and their needs can be met by natural light from your windows or artificial light.

Fluorescent light (two tubes) is a good choice. It produces less heat than an ordinary light bulb (heat is harmful and can dry out your plant) and is very efficient for plant nurturing and growth. You can get away with the standard fluorescent lights such as "cool white" although the grow-type units (Grow Lux and Verilux are trade names, and I especially like Verilux) do provide a better color spectrum coverage. Increased red spectrum can help speed growth and flowering in some plant varieties. A point to remember: Grow-type units are generally close to twice the cost of a standard fluorescent light and for most people probably aren't necessary. But

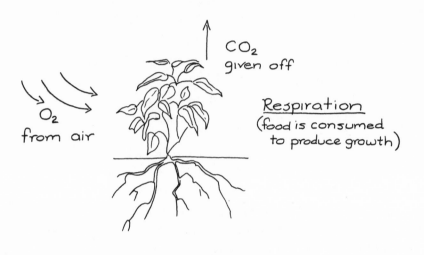

O_2 from air

CO_2 given off

<u>Respiration</u>
(food is consumed to produce growth)

$$O_2 \;+\; \text{Plant Sugar}$$

Respiration

if you do want the *greatest* amount of blooms, largest size, top quality—then get the growlights. *Tip*: You can intensify your light by using a white reflector around the fluorescent tubes, thus throwing the light down toward the plants.

So, for the eight-foot by three-foot workbench, you can use one fixture with two fluorescent bulbs and provide adequate light. For the equivalent of very bright sunlight that will be needed for your flowering plants, you may want to add two fixtures over the bench and have the output of four fluorescent bulbs. Another option and less costly than two fixtures is a high-output (HO) fluorescent fixture,

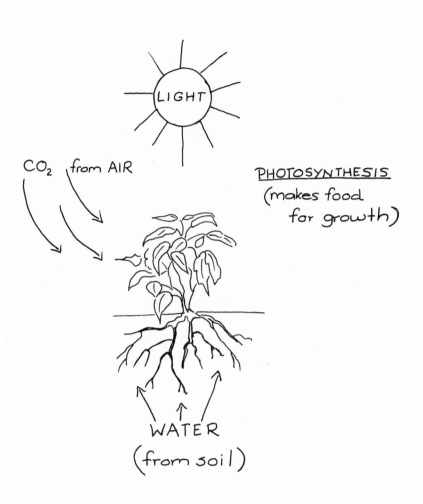

WATER + CO₂ + LIGHT

Photosynthesis

which puts out greater light or foot candles. These units are available at electrical supply outlets.

To simulate and/or control daylight for your plants you will need an automatic timer. In this way you can shorten the daylight during winter to give them a rest period, and then increase the light during the growing period to stimulate growth and bring about flowering.

Figure on sixteen to eighteen hours of artificial light during the peak growing periods. This can be cut back to ten to twelve hours during the winter. Leave them at this ten-to-twelve-hour cycle for three or four months and then gradually increase an hour or so once a month until you reach the sixteen-to-eighteen-hour period of artificial light time. Remember that plants need darkness for rest as you do.

If you want to get away from the flowering pattern of your particular climate, there is another option available to you as a plant pet owner in control of his pets: You can do it by varying your fluorescent light! By lengthening the hours of light at an odd season you will be able to start growth and flowering.

If your Living Quarters are large or you have more than one area set aside for Living Quarters you may want to have two timers in order to achieve different seasons or different amounts of daylight for each area. As you experiment with your lights and your plants you will discover for yourself the unlimited options you have. With a little practice you will be able to have a series of blooming plants through the coldest, darkest winter.

If fluorescent bulbs seem too fancy for you, don't be concerned, incandescent lights will also work, and there are row-type versions of regular lights. Just remember that they do give off heat and therefore the plants will require more watering.

NEXT STEP—INSTALLATION

What we're after here for your plants is consistent lighting of their Living Quarters. Fluorescent lights are available in both short and long lengths and circular patterns. So if you have constructed the four- or eight-foot-long bench discussed earlier then a four- or eight-foot-long light fixture is what you want.

Where to find: Bulbs and fixture can be purchased at most hardware and electrical supply houses. Some units come with a shade around the lights, which focuses the energy and intensity downward toward the plants. This is desirable but not necessary.

Attach your lights to the ceiling with hook and chain or any other changeable cord to allow you to vary the height of the lights. Depending upon what stage your plants are in you will need flexibility with your lighting arrangements. Flowering plants will require substantial light to bloom, so you will need to lower your light to within a foot or two of the top of the plants. Other plants will only need a light source two to four feet from the top of their heads. You can move fluorescent lights to within six inches of your plants for maximum light without damage. For increased intensity use more than one fixture over a given workbench or tray.

Remember that most plants tolerate a large range of light and still produce good growth and flowering. If you do find that one of your plant pets is not flowering, just move it closer to a greater light source. Lighting is as complicated and as simple as that!

TYPICAL PLANT BOOK INSTRUCTIONS FOR LIGHTING AND TEMPERATURE

	Light	*Temperature*
Hoya or wax plant	Slightly shady	Warm, 55° minimum
Episcia or flame violet	Shady	Warm, 60° to 70°
Spider plant	Shade or sun	Moderate, 50° to 70° at night
Swedish ivy	Bright light	Warm
Beefsteak begonia	Bright light but not full sun	Warm, 60° to 70° at night
Jade plant	Full sun or shade	Warm, 50° to 60° at night
Velvet plant	Bright but not more than early morning or late afternoon sun	Warm, 60° to 70° at night
Christmas cactus	Bright light	Warm but cooler to set blooms
Gardenia	Bright light but screen from direct sun	Warm, 60° to 70° at night
Hibiscus	Full sun	Warm, 60° to 70° at night, cooler in winter

Citrus	Sun or light shade	Moderate, 50° to 60° at night
Corn plant	Well-lighted but no direct sun	Warm, 60° to 70° at night
Ficus or weeping fig	Good light but never full sun	Warm, 60° to 70° at night
Peperomia or radiator plant	Bright light, no direct sun	Warm, 60° to 70° at night
Bromeliad or rainbow star	Slight shade	Warm, 60° to 70° at night
Lady slipper orchid	Semi-shade	Warm
Moth orchid	Shady	Warm, 60° to 70° at night

Air

Air is as essential to your plants as it is to you, but when we say "air" for plants we are talking about carbon dioxide. As we discussed in the lighting section, plants need carbon dioxide to produce carbohydrates (sugar) for energy; this process releases oxygen (a benefit for you) into the air.

Terrific, you say, but where am I going to get carbon dioxide for my plants? No problem. Not only is there CO_2 in the air, but you as a breathing human provide CO_2 every time you exhale.

Air movement is helpful to your plant pets, but not essential. In very humid conditions, it helps to reduce fungus problems.

So, how do you make the air move? Just get an ordinary, everyday fan and place it where it will circulate the air under your plants' Living Quarters or over the top of your plants. The idea is not to blow air directly on the plants but just to keep air circulating.

Temperature and Humidity

Now that you have the CO_2 requirements satisfied you'll want to provide the correct temperature for your plant pet. I know you've heard about cool-growing plants. There are also intermediate-, hot-, or warm-growing plants, and plants that prefer dry, moist, or humid conditions. You probably thought what a complicating, confusing jungle of information to plough through. It doesn't have to be so. Your pet bird may have come from a very moist, steamy jungle but does very well in your house which has varied temperatures and humidity. Dogs bred in the cold Northwest, such as the huskie, still do well in warmer climates. Just remember what I told you about your plant pets earlier. They are not fragile, they want to survive. They can and will adapt to the different temperatures and humidity of your house . . . gradually. They need time to adjust.

Most plants originated in warm areas like Central or South America and were used to humidity and warmth, but despite that they have a greater tolerance for temperature changes than most plant books or flower shops will tell you.

In Appendix IV you will find a table of plants with their groupings and preferences for humidity and temperature. This table reflects the suggested ideal conditions as described in plant reference books.

What does this mean to you? It means that if your plant had its druthers it would prefer to grow in the general conditions shown in the table . . . but it will live very well in conditions you establish in the plant's Living Quarters.

For example, the orchid family has members that grow under many conditions. The cymbidium is a cool-growing variety; the cattleya is intermediate; and the vanda is warm-growing. Yet, these three orchids can be successfully grown in the same Living Quarters because plants can take a greater humidity and temperature range than the table or most books would suggest.

The jade plant, hoya, or bromeliad plants—and most others on the chart—will live and thrive in most areas.

So set up your Living Quarters with the knowledge that you will be able to house a large variety of plants without worrying about changing the air, light, or temperature to fit each one's "preference." If you were to peek into my Living Quarters you'd find all of the plants I've just mentioned living quite healthily and happily. So far, none of them has complained and it's been ten years of peaceful coexistence in the basement—60-70 degrees in the winter and 70-80 degrees in summer.

This ten degree difference between the seasons may not sound like much but it is important because your plant pet needs this change to start the bloom process. Another factor is length of days, so for blooming plants follow this chart:

	TEMPERATURE	LIGHT
Winter	60-70 degrees	12-14 hours
Summer	70-80 degrees	16-18 hours

Still no blooms? Change the conditions. Try shortening the light in winter and lengthening it in summer (use a timer on your fluorescent bulbs). Change the temperature in winter to provide a sharper contrast to summer by leaving the window open. Increase the intensity of light by moving it closer to the source. A lot of information but a very simple procedure.

If your plants' Living Quarters are not in the basement, what can you do about a plant pet who is rather pokey about blooming? Experiment and see what happens. Bathroom Living Quarters? Open a window slightly and that will change the temperature. Humidity problem? Leave some water in the tub. Light? Lengthen or shorten days by using a timer attached to fluorescent bulbs.

Keep in mind that the humidity-temperature range you're aiming for is an intermediate zone of thirty to fifty degrees relative humidity and sixty to seventy degrees temperatures. If you can't get this exactly, don't fret—your plants will still do well.

Having a number of plants growing together in your Living Quarters automatically creates more humidity. Humidity produced this way is called the transpiration process (it's a lot easier to understand than photosynthesis and you mastered that!). Transpiration is similar to our perspiring, only plants

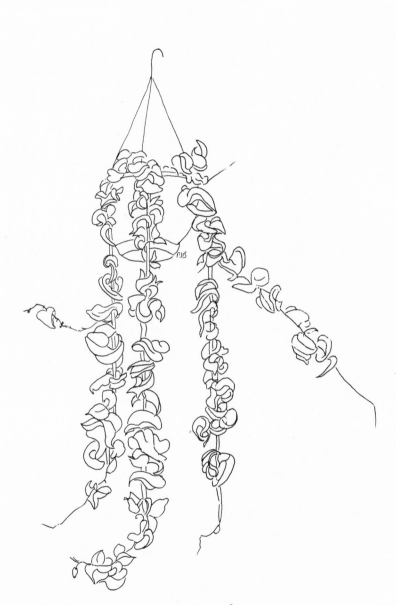

Hoya or wax plant

release their moisture through their leaves. Humidity is increased as this moisture evaporates into the air. Check the humidity level whenever you see your plant pet's leaves drooping or wilted; could be that your plant is in an area where there is rapidly moving hot or dry air—this will cause your pet to lose moisture faster than it can replace it through its roots. See illustration:

So if you have five, ten, or twenty plants lounging in the Living Quarters they are producing humidity—no charge to you. It's been pointed out that there is nothing harder than growing a single plant in a living room and nothing easier than growing twenty plants in their Living Quarters.

The reason? When you get that many plants together you are recreating nature's conditions and you can't do better than that.

You're really the wizard in charge of Living Quarters environment. With a flick of the switch you control air movement, you create temperature changes with a furnace, a heater, or by opening a window or a door. Does the humidity need altering? Add more water to the basement floor or fill up the tub (bathroom Living Quarters).

You'll find that spending time with your pets in their Living Quarters is fun. Statistics are not in on whether plant pet owners look younger than animal pet owners but one thing is sure—a few hours spent in your plant pets' Living Quarters will do a lot more for you than the same time spent in the doghouse.

Once you've got your Living Quarters set up

Beefsteak begonia

you're really on your way. Now you have a place to put new plant pets instead of plopping them on a windowsill or table and hoping for the best. It's a great place to send your underachievers (bloom-wise). Pack them off to Living Quarters and let them luxuriate in the climate, light, and moisture and pretty soon they'll be blooming prettily again.

5
Housebreaking

You've got your plant, established its Living Quarters, know the basics about light-air-humidity-temperature. You are now ready to tackle housebreaking. No snickers, please, housebreaking is important.

A bird has it's cage—little housebreaking here; once you've bought your fish and put him in his bowl he is set, but a dog and cat have to be trained to use paper, litter box, and finally the great outdoors. What, I hear you ask, do I do with a plant? Your plant pet will have to be trained to use its new pot and soil—this is what you are going to teach him.

When you buy your pet keep it in its old pot at first. Moving is always a shock to the plant's system because there is an abrupt change in air, temperature, humidity, and light. That's why it will be reassuring to your plant to find as he's transported to his new home that his "feet" are still in the same old slippers.

When you notice that your plant pet has outgrown its pot (roots sticking through the bottom), or that the soil has deteriorated and is waterlogged, or that your plant came bare rooted (without the pot); or that you can't stand the pot—then go ahead and start his training—but do it gently. Check the following pot and soil basics before you begin.

The Pot Story

You won't kill your plant pet if you pick the wrong pot; Rocky will do well in almost anything. Base the decision on *your* needs: How often will you be watering your plant? How do you want the plant and its pot to fit in your decorating scheme? All kinds of pots are available to complement any home, and you may want to look at several home and garden magazines for ideas.

Here are some things to think about:

1. Do you want a pot that will help you train your pet to your schedule?
2. Do you want a pot that will provide the optimum chance for your pet plant's growth?
3. Do you want a pot that will fit into your plant's Living Quarters so you can water all the plants *at once*, preferably every three to four days? *Note:* Don't come up with a complicated watering schedule that depends on you to remember if the jade plant gets watered on Tuesday, does the hibiscus get watered on Wednesday?

What is your schedule? When is it convenient for you to water your plants? At what intervals? A three-to-four-day interval provides a nice balance of pot and soil conditions. You could extend this cycle for five days or even once a week with only a few restrictions on the number of plant varieties you can grow successfully.

Learn the watering requirements of your plant pet. Check a reference book to see whether your plant likes to be pot-bound. This means growing a plant in a very small container so that the roots are bunched together to encourage blooming. The Clivia plant, for example, loves a tight situation like this.

Look at the root structure and compare it to the size of the foliage. Let's say you need a three-to-four-day watering cycle (you're very busy and you don't have time to be running around with a watering can every other day), your plant to be potted is a large plant with lots of foliage (two feet tall and one foot in diameter), and the plant also needs damp growing conditions. This means the pot you are looking for should be two inches larger around the sides than the root ball, a little on the deep side, and the pot should be made of plastic as opposed to clay.

Why? Because the combination of a plastic pot with a larger quantity of soil will keep the soil damp between watering periods. If the plant is damp, it doesn't need to be watered, and your time is your own. You have a housebroken plant that is adapting to your schedule. And you did it just by juggling the type and size of the pot, the size of the plant, and the watering frequency.

What if the plant pet you picked needs a dry period between watering? Then pick a clay pot. Moisture evaporates very quickly through clay and your plant will not remain damp. So a two-foot-tall plant with a one-foot diameter could live very happily in a clay pot six inches in diameter.

If the root ball of any plant is bigger than the pot, don't throw the pot away, just cut away some of the roots with a knife and make the plant fit the container.

THE GREAT POT-SIZE CONTROVERSY

Generally, your plant pet will fare better if the pot size is slightly larger than the existing root ball (one-half inch to one inch around the sides). If it is any bigger you'll need more soil and that will slow down the drying-out process.

As you thumb through reference books you may find that they recommend a pot-bound condition for your plant pet if you want blooms. If a plant is pot-bound it is difficult to keep its roots moist (because there is less soil around those roots), and the plant will dry out faster. The only thing I can tell you is that I have grown many plants that the books indicate should be pot-bound and I have not supplied this condition—and the plants still bloomed.

If you want to try the pot-bound approach to generate blooming, then use a plastic pot to retain moisture and you can water on your three-to-four-day cycle.

If you have the time for more frequent watering or for individual watering, your pot can be tailored to your pet's needs, and you might want to choose the clay pot. As the clay breathes, the soil will dry out, and air will get to your plant's roots. This will mean more frequent watering but your plant will benefit from the watering/drying-out process.

If your Living Quarters has relatively high humidity—50 degrees or above—the soil will not dry out as fast and your plant will not need frequent watering. So you can afford to choose a smaller size pot and still meet your watering schedule of every three to four days.

On the other hand, if you have a dry growing area—thirty degrees relative humidity or less—the soil will lose moisture more quickly so you will have to go to a bigger pot to meet your schedule.

One more thing—a plant endowed with a lot of foliage will use more water than a semi-bald plant.

At this point you probably feel as if all this information should be fed into a computer—size of foliage, size and type of pot, watering frequency, air temperature—but as you work with your plant pets you'll hit on the right balance almost automatically. And believe me, they'll work with you until you do.

Soil

Soil is a major character in your plant pet's life. Soil allows moisture, nutrition, and air to reach the plant's roots, while holding those roots firm and supporting the plant—preferably in an upright, nonwobbly position.

Most gardening books suggest you use different soil mixtures for each plant variety. Usually a combination of peat moss, sand, and potting soil; or topsoil, humus, and soil conditioners (vermiculite, perlite, charcoal particles). For example:

SOIL MIXTURES GRADED BY TEXTURE

Compact	Fine sand
Semi-compact	1 part sandy loam, 1 part peat
Regular	1 part sandy loam, 1 part peat, 1 part sawdust
Very porous	2 parts peat, 1 part sharp builder's sand
Loose	1 part sandy loam, 1 part peat, 1 part coarse perlite

DEFINITIONS

Perlite	White, volcanic rock that will not decompose. Provides aeration to potting mixtures
Builder's sand	Washed; free of organic matter
Beach sand	Too fine and salty unless washed
Peat moss	Light brown and acid. Retains moisture

You can fuss with all these combinations, offer them to your plant pets, and find they respond enthusiastically, just as your dog would if you offered him filet mignon. But the truth is your dog will do great on dog food and your plant pets will thrive on common potting soil. You can even use topsoil from your yard if you sterilize it by heating first. I would stick with the potting soil. It's not expensive and you don't really want to spend precious time cooking dirt in your oven.

Buy potting soil in large twenty-five to fifty-pound plastic bags. Be sure to get some perlite to mix with the soil. Perlite (see table, p. 46) keeps the potting soil from compacting or getting waterlogged. It also encourages air circulation through the roots.

Soil recipe for plants that need moist growing conditions: Mix potting soil with a small amount of perlite, five parts soil to one part perlite. If the soil does not stay moist between the three-to-four-day waterings then leave out the perlite. You could add peat moss or vermiculite to the soil, but only if you're planning to extend your watering schedule to one week.

Soil recipe for plants that need dry growing conditions: For plants that need dry conditions, use equal parts potting soil with perlite. For plants that need very dry conditions, like cactus, add ordinary sand to the mixture—one part potting soil with one part perlite and one part sand.

Soil recipe for plants that like normal growing conditions: Follow this combination for most plants: two parts potting soil and one part perlite. This mixture will be great for the plants that love to dry out between watering periods (and that's most plants). This will fit in nicely with the three-to-four-day watering schedule.

Acid, neutral, alkali, PH scale? What's it all about?

Maybe you've been reading that it is important to pay attention to the soil's condition. Is it acid, neutral, or alkali? This is called the PH scale. A rate of

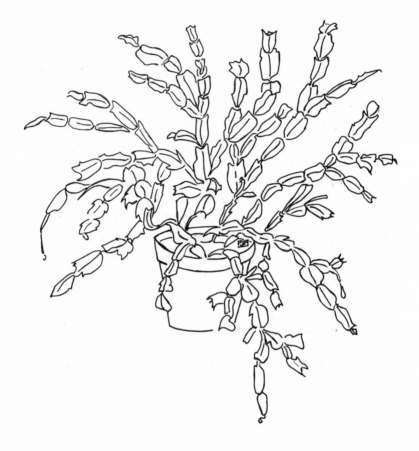

Christmas cactus

six to seven means the soil is neutral, everything below this indicates an acid condition. If the rate is above six to seven, your soil is probably alkali. If you want to determine the PH of your soil you will need a soil-testing kit. Then, depending upon what you find, you can add materials like limestone (neutralizes an acid condition and moves the soil to an alkaline state) or cottonseed meal (moves alkaline soil to a more acid state).

But don't worry. If all this creates an image in your mind of a mad scientist clutching his soil-testing kit and up to his eyeballs in various kinds of soil, you really don't *have* to do this step at all. Most plants, Rocky included, will grow in good old everyday common potting soil. In fact, standard potting soil approximates a reasonable PH for a wide variety of plants.

And don't be afraid, as you try different soil/water combinations and your pet wheezes and gurgles through the dry and wet extremes, that you're about to be the owner of an ex-plant pet. Your plant will hang in there until you hit on the right soil/water balance for both of you. Once your pet has adapted to the pot and soil, his leaves shiny, his posture perky, he is housebroken. And just like house broken dogs and cats, a housebroken plant pet is the only kind to have.

Purple velvet plant

6
Food and Drink

Food

You've probably been feeding a dog, a cat, or a bird. Feeding a plant pet is similar but not as time-consuming. Your plant pet won't sit up and beg for fattening scraps from the table and you *won't* have to feed it every day (the way you would a dog or cat).

Plants get their nutrition from the soil—breakfast, lunch, dinner, and dessert. Good soil has minerals, phosphoric acid, and potash, which the plant needs. So if the soil is good, chock-full of nutrients, your plant's menu needs nothing added. However, most plants benefit from a moderate feeding of fertilizer.

There are special fertilizers available for certain plant families but you don't need to use them; your pet will do fine with a simple all-purpose formula because all fertilizers, special or otherwise, contain

sufficient nitrogen and other ingredients to pro-
mote growth and blooms.

A FEW BASIC FERTILIZER FACTS

What do you know about fertilizers? They come in
bags, boxes, bottles, etc., with various formulas
printed on the front in big block letters—a confusing picture to the new plant pet owner. But just as
you don't have to be a veterinarian to feed your dog,
you don't have to be a chemist to feed your plants—it
only looks that way.

There are two kinds of fertilizers: (1) *Organic*—
manure, sawdust, and leaf mold, all of which decom-
pose slowly. (2) *Inorganic,* which is chemical. All inorganic fertilizers contain nitrogen, which stimulates
foliage; phosphorus, which strengthens roots; and
potassium, which encourages blooms. Organic fertilizers are more difficult to use, harder to find, and
often more costly than the inorganic types.

Let's look at the inorganic fertilizers. The ones
with the strange formulas that look like football
plays, 12-8-4, 8-4-2. They all contain several basic
ingredients—nitrogen, phosphorus, potassium.
These elements are always listed on the label as a
percent which represents the concentration of each
ingredient. So, when you read a label that says
12-8-4, this means the fertilizer contains 12 percent
nitrogen, 8 percent phosphorus, and 4 percent potassium. The balance may differ from fertilizer to
fertilizer, but nitrogen will usually be the major ingredient.

The special-formula fertilizers are used for plants like azaleas or gardenias to meet these plants' acidity needs. Special fertilizers are also available for roses, orchids, and other plant groups. You will never need to bother with all the various special fertilizers offered, but they are there if you want them.

What you will need to use when feeding Rocky is your common sense. Think about the way you feed your dog. He gets sick when you feed him too much and scrawny when you feed him too little. Your plant reacts in the same way.

SOME TIPS ON FERTILIZING

1. *Do not overfeed.* Overfeeding (too frequently and too much) will give Rocky that old scraggly look—extended or weakened stems and leaves. Also, fertilizer can build up in the soil creating a salt toxicity that will convince your plant you're trying to poison him. You can water very heavily *once in a while* to flush the soil and get rid of the salt buildup.

2. *Follow the directions on the label (almost).* I recommend using less than the suggested dose. Try half the amount and save yourself some money. Fertilize once every month instead of every two weeks and save yourself some time.

3. *When plants are inactive cut back on food.* If your dog is not getting exercise you cut back on his food so he won't get fat and sluggish. Plants' low exercise (slow growth) periods are during the winter months because of the shorter daylight hours. During this time fertilize only every two months.

4. *Fertilize the soil, not the leaves.* It's believed that plants can take nutrients through their leaves but the purpose of fertilizing is to encourage the root system, not the foliage. Liquid fertilizer is easy to apply and its strength can be controlled; granular fertilizer, designed to be placed on the soil and eventually break down is fine, just don't use too much.

If you can't remember all the fertilizer facts, just remember this: Use a balanced, all-purpose fertilizer, follow the manufacturer's suggestions (but at a slightly lower strength and frequency), and use your common sense. You won't make any irreversible mistakes; in fact you can forget to feed your plants for six months or even a year and they will still be alive when you get around to it.

Water

Watering is a mysterious rite for most plant owners. They look at the plant—does it seem a little dry or hot? How about squirting, spraying, pouring on a little water? Is the plant not growing fast enough? You guessed it, they water again. The plant, roots awash in an accumulated sea, finally drowns and the plant owner shakes his head and says, "I guess I didn't water enough."

Why will overwatering kill your plant? Outside plants can survive a veritable deluge of continuous rain; they will also do well during long, dry spells. But these plants in nature are usually growing where there is good drainage, so their roots get air and never get saturated, even during periods of constant rain.

Nature has provided outdoor plants with an ability to take dry periods too. Look at your grass during a very hot, parched summer. It seems brown and dead but after a jolt of rain it revives and turns green.

So, you're convinced, plants outside are durable and can stand extremes. Then why won't they do the same thing in your house?

They can. If you miss a watering or two your plant may give a good impersonation of a dying, wilting plant but it will rally when water arrives. Ironically, there is less danger to your plants if you are a forgetful plant owner than a zealous one.

However, an indoor plant can survive overwatering if there is good drainage and periods where the soil gets a chance to dry out. Some plants, like the gardenia, appreciate nothing better than staying semi-wet all day, but most plants, given that treatment, will just turn up their roots and gasp for a life preserver.

I made the same mistake we all make. I felt very responsible for my plants' survival, so every time I passed Gloria the gloxinia or Sven the Swedish ivy, I poured another pitcher of water on their heads. When in doubt, water your plants, right? Sven and Gloria soon passed on to that great jungle in the sky, glug-glugging all the way. So I found through many years of trial and error and many hours of conversation with plant store owners that *drainage is the key.*

SOME TIPS ON WATERING

1. *A pot without a drainage hole* is bad news for your plants. The soil looks dry but watch out, it can be sopping and saturated on the bottom. But, you protest, those clay pots with the drainage holes will look gross in my living room. You can solve your decor and drainage problems at the same time; just put your pot with drainage hole into an attractive planter. Check from time to time to make sure no water is building up in the decorator pot.

2. *You've got to get that plant out of that pot—occasionally.* Nothing lasts forever and neither will your soil. After a few years in the same old pot it will begin to break down and compact. Then you'll have soggy soil and your plant will have perpetually wet feet. Transplant your pet every two to three years, throw out the old soil and replace it.

3. *Water, water, everywhere, I think I'm going to sink.* Repeat this a hundred times: *I will not overwater.* I will let my plants dry out from top to bottom (make this pledge yearly).

If you do overwater for a week or a month, give your plant a chance to dry out. Unfortunately, those of you who haven't kicked the watering-can habit can't seem to stop long enough for the drying-out period.

4. *Soil that needs aeration is no fun for plants to sit in.* Hard, claylike soil may be great material for mud pies but it's terrible for your plants. Repot!

5. *Are you overwatering during humid, cold periods?*

Doesn't even sound right, does it? When it's cold and humid plants retain moisture. Sharply reduce watering frequency—save time and your plant.

6. *Don't let your plant pot sit in a saucer or tray filled with water.* The idea is good, a saucer to collect excess water from the drainage hole, but pour off the water—just don't let it sit around. Roots need to dry out or they'll rot. Except for the gardenia, which likes to stay damp, your plants will be better off if you put them and their pots in a tray filled with pebbles; water collecting in the tray will add moisture to the air and not to the roots.

As an ex-overwaterer I know telling you to stop overwatering is easier than doing it. But it should help to remember that if your plant really needs water it will tell you. Try these tests:

1. Are the leaves wilting, is the soil dry, are there cracks between the soil and the pot?
2. Does the soil look and feel dry?
3. What kind of pot is your plant in? Clay pots make soil dry out faster. Plastic pots help soil retain water longer.
4. What is the pot size? A small plant in a large pot isn't watered as often as a large plant in a small pot.
5. Consider the weather conditions. Is it cold? Are there short sunlight days? Is the atmosphere humid? Then skip a watering.

Still not sure? Try this next:

1. Lift up the pot. Is it heavier or lighter than

usual? A pot filled with soil saturated with water feels heavy, If so, *don't water.*

2. Insert a thin steel wire (or pencil) into the soil. If the bottom of the wire is damp, *don't water.*
3. Buy a moisture indicator. If the meter (which is attached to a rod in the soil) reads wet . . . *don't water.*

You won't have to make all these tests before you water your plant pet; just one should do if you think Rocky is drying out too much. If the test shows the soil is wet, recheck in a few days to see when it finally dries. If it dries in less than a week, water your plant on the revised schedule. If it takes longer than a week to dry out, get rid of the soil and transplant.

Establish a watering schedule that is convenient for you. Your dog might enjoy snacking every few hours but you don't drop whatever you're doing to accommodate him. And he is healthier on few and regular meals. He adapts to your schedule and Rocky will too.

WATER MORE	WATER LESS FREQUENTLY
1. On hot, sunny days	1. On rainy, dark days
2. On windy days	2. In cool, damp weather
3. If the plants require high humidity or moist growth	3. Plants that prefer dry conditions
4. During a period of active growth	4. Plants not growing or dormant
5. Plants with large leaves and a mass of foliage.	

What about misting?

You can mist your plants but it is not necessary. It does reduce leaf temperature, lowers rate of transpiration so the plant will require less watering, but misting takes time; one more job for you to think about. Why not skip it, your plants won't complain.

Give Your Plant a Bath

Now that you are a reformed overwaterer you may want to do another favor for your plant—give it a bath. Your plant pet will enjoy this and can be counted upon to sit still and not shake water all over you and the rug.

Bathing will wash dust off the leaves, allowing them to do a better job taking in CO_2. Try bathing your plant every three or four months, or if that's inconvenient, once a year. Wait a minute—don't fill up the tub and submerge your pet. When I say "bath" I'm really talking about a good, thorough spraying with lukewarm water (add one teaspoon of a mild detergent to one quart of water if you have insect problems).

Put Rocky in a sink or bathtub and spray his leaves briskly, both sides if possible. No commercial cleaners are necessary. If Rocky is a plant with hairy leaves skip the bath and mist, using a soft brush to get him clean.

What about hard water or soft water? Will my plant know the difference? He will if your water has gone through a softening process. Sodium (salt) is a water softener and salt and plants do not mix. If your whole house is tied into the system, look for a watering tank or faucet outlet *before* the water reaches the softening process. There is usually a faucet at the bottom of the tank. Attach a small hose to the faucet and this can be your watering source. Fill up your watering pitcher here. No faucet? Then turn the system off. You should let the water run a few minutes to clear the softened water from the pipes.

This may sound extreme, but if neither option is available to you how about having a plumber install a faucet between the tank and the softener system? Not only will your plants perk up, but you may too. Salt is not good for humans either.

7
Grooming

Have you ever bought a plant based on looks alone? Maybe you espied it across the supermarket floor, ablaze with blooms and thought, "That plant is gorgeous. I'll take it home, put it on the coffee table, and no one will notice the couch needs cleaning." Now, one year later, the plant is alive, but no longer on the coffee table. It's been banished to a corner because its foliage is growing in all directions; one side seems to be flourishing more than the other. The plant has developed a very "goofy" quality. In fact, you've decided to toss it. . . .

Wait! All your plant needs is a little grooming, a little attention to restore it to the blooming belle it once was. And an important part of grooming is pruning.

Pruning

I know pruning seems difficult. You think it will hurt the plant; you're afraid you won't do it right. But understand that your plant can be transformed, with pruning, from an ugly, overgrown plant (about to be liquidated) into a beautiful, cherished plant pet. Be honest, isn't it easier to love your dog when he looks clean, de-fleaed, shampooed, combed, and smelling good? The same is true for your plant.

First, realize that pruning is a natural and necessary process for plant development. In nature there are many pruning agents and none do it very gently. Storms break off plants' branches, birds and animals chew on their foliage. This keeps the plant compact and encourages strong branch formation. Now your plant, no longer under nature's care, needs to be pruned by you. Here's why:

If you cut back a branch, this causes the branch to divide into two or more growths at the point of the cut. Why is this good? It enhances beauty and health. Some plants like the hibiscus tend to grow straight up (stalklike). When you cut back you cause branching. This gives the plant a fuller, rounded look and increases the branches' strength as well. Pruning takes the plant back to a manageable size.

Outside, the citrus, hibiscus, and gardenia can grow to bush size. That's why, in your home, they can, in a short time, outgrow their space. And we've all seen what plants (and people) look like when that happens. There's nothing worse than a plant grow-

Hibiscus

ing up around the ceiling with very little foliage around its base.

Another candidate for pruning is the plant with branches leaning so far to one side that it needs support from strings or sticks to keep it from breaking off. Or that hanging pot that once looked so lush and now just has a few spindly branches weakly crawling over the edge of the pot, with all the growth below.

Pruning lets you eliminate an odd branch or growth—growths that are growing out of proportion to the rest of the plant or in a direction you think is misguided. Often a plant will develop new shoots that grow helter-skelter, ruining the plant's outline. With pruning you can bring back its shape and strengthen the shoots.

PRUNING LESSON

1. Don't cut off the tip of a branch. This will produce new growth at the end of the tip, placing additional weight on the original branch. New growth here is what makes the plant look "goofy."
2. *Before cutting,* decide on the overall appearance or shape you feel would look good on your plant.
3. Then cut far enough down on the original plant to get branching, compact growth, and a strong plant. Cut back far enough so that the new growth will be supported on a strong branch or trunk. Really cut away; don't be

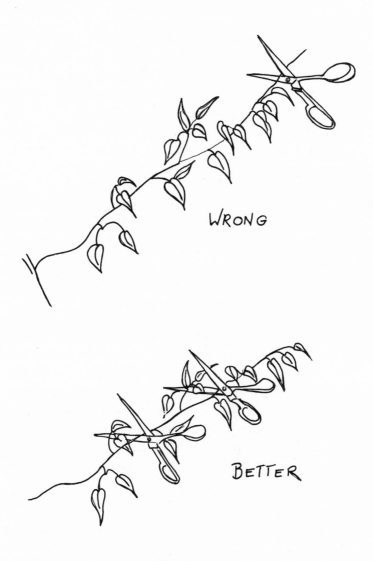

WRONG

BETTER

Pruning

afraid. The plant will benefit and look better than ever.

4. Don't expect instant beauty when you cut way back. The plant may not look company-pretty for a while—somewhat like a poodle that's just been sheared. As soon as new growth develops you'll be a pruning believer.

5. Try to avoid cutting back all the foliage. Make your cut above the last one or two leaves—counting from the base, not the tip.

6. When should one cut all the way back? When your plant has grown very "leggy"—to the ceiling with only a few leaves at the top. Your plant will survive a deep cut and send out new growth from the base which will eventually turn into beautiful foliage. A leggy and unattractive plant will benefit from pruning.

7. Prune after the blooming season, usually spring. This is when new growth develops; especially the gardenia, hybiscus, and citrus. The vine-type plants—Swedish ivy or the velvet plant—can be clipped any time.

8. Prune every year or two instead of waiting for a Neanderthal bush plant to develop. It's easier on the plant to get a light haircut every so often instead of major surgery.

A pruning bonus: You can use the cutting to produce new plants.

Final word: Pruning is an important factor in plant pet care success. It is often avoided; when it is, your plants will look sloppy, like a dog without a bath or combing. If you remember "less watering, more pruning" you'll have the best looking pets on the block.

Training

Training is the "show-clipping" part of grooming. And like clipping a poodle, it's a kind of art that gives plants a stylized shape or form. More compact, slow-growing plants usually don't require much shaping and are hard to train, but fast-growing shrubs or vines respond very well, and the training process can add greatly to their beauty.

SIMPLE TRAINING

The idea is to train the plant's growth the way you want it. Let your vine grow up a lattice by tying the new growth to the latticework, and watching it take on a particular shape.

Or tie your shrub to a stick and let it follow a pattern, or wire the branches to force their growth in a certain direction.

The illustration on page 68 shows you how.

EXOTIC TRAINING

You can also do very imaginative things with your plant, like potting two or three young hibiscus plants together, with the plants' trunks woven around each other to form a braided effect. Once you have inter-

Training

woven the two, three, or four, depending upon the number of branches you use, they will in time grow together and form a very interesting pattern.

Be creative when you groom—don't be timid. Experiment freely. Plants, like other pets, respond well to grooming and you can produce very unusual and beautiful effects.

Grooming tip: You may read or be told that various chemical sprays should be used on your plant to add a shine or brilliance to its foliage. Don't bother. This is time-consuming, not necessarily good for your plants, and a costly way to accomplish the same results you'd get with water.

Repotting

This is your chance to play with your plant pet at a time you choose. Repotting is part of good grooming for your plant and relaxing for you—there's something calming about working with plants and soil. It's a nice respite if you have a busy life.

How will you know if it's time to repot? Look at your plant. A few stray roots do not mean that repotting is needed. Are the roots snaking out of the pot—either through the drainage hole or over the top? If so, don't panic. This is not an emergency situation; your tough little plant pet can go for months, years even, with his feet hanging out of his house. But Rocky *will* look a lot better and welcome additional soil for his roots if you fix him up.

Repot if the soil has broken down and is saturated. You'll remember the saturated soil story from our discussion on watering. It usually happens in a large pot (eight inches or more in diameter). Repot as soon as possible—there is a chance the root structure will rot if you don't.

Do you have a thirsty plant that wants to be watered soon after it's been watered? The thirsty-plant syndrome happens when a plant becomes very big and outgrows the pot. If your plant and pot are constantly falling over (due to large plant/small pot) and your plant does have a drinking problem, then it is time to find a larger pot.

Have you repotted your plant in the last three or four years? If not, you should. Nothing lasts forever, including the nutrients in your pet's soil.

Okay, you agree, my plant's roots are climbing up the walls and I know it's time to repot. What happens next?

Get in some comfortable work clothes, have on hand scissors to cut back dead roots, and a cardboard box for debris. Find a place where you won't worry about dirt spilling on the floor—your plant's Living Quarters, or a garage, basement, or out in your yard, or a newspaper spread on your kitchen floor.

Many plant books will devote chapters to the proper, precise way to transplant and how to set the roots just so in the new soil. If you have time and want to follow these detailed instructions you can; but believe me, you really don't have to take on this extra work.

Just do the following for successful repotting:

1. Remove the old pot by tapping the side with your palm; this loosens the root ball from the pot. Lift the plant out. Don't be afraid—you will not hurt the plant. If the plant does not come out easily, then turn the plant upside down and tap the top rim of the pot on a bench or table until the ball loosens. When you turn the pot upside down, soil may spill out—use your cardboard box to catch this soil; you can throw it away later.

2. Remove the old root ball with as little disturbance to the soil and roots as possible. Do this over the cardboard box. If the soil falls away, look at the exposed dead roots and if rotted cut them. The soil most often falls away if it is water-saturated, which could produce root rot. Don't worry if you lose a lot of the soil and the roots are disturbed. The plant will take slightly longer to adjust, but will do fine. Finally, if the root system is pot-bound, take a knife and cut the surface of the root ball no more than 1/8″ deep down the side every ninety degrees and across the bottom. This will stimulate the roots to send out root growth into the new soil at the cut points.

3. Next, take the root ball and put it in a pot with the plant sunk in the new soil at the same level as before. The soil level should be one-half to one inch below the rim of the pot to allow for easier watering. Add your soil (you've already mixed the soil with inert material for drainage

Repotting

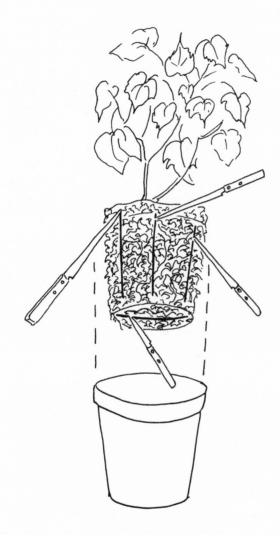

Cutting a root ball

and aeration) around the side of the pot until it is filled. Press down hard on the soil so that the plant is secure and the soil along the sides is all the way down in the pot. Another way is to tap the bottom of the pot on the bench or the floor. This will settle the soil around the roots without damaging them.

4. The soil you use for repotting should be moist, but this is not essential if you don't want to bother. You can add water right in the pot to secure the soil and give Rocky the moisture he needs, and he will want a lot right after transplanting.

You have just made your first plant pet transplanting operation and I know it will be successful. Your plant will need some time to adjust to its new home. Its root system has been disturbed and rest is in order. Just as your dog would lie down for a rest after a long exercise period, your plant should have reduced activity for a week or so until the roots can regain their strength. For a plant, light produces activity and the brighter the light the more activity and demand on the root system. That's why, after transplanting, I suggest you keep your plant in a spot with less light for a week or two.

If you are contemplating transplanting an orchid the procedure is still the same even though the orchid plant's requirements are slightly different. The orchid prefers to grow in fern fiber or fir bark and is mainly an air plant that, in nature, attaches itself to a tree. It receives its nutrition from water and air, not

Moth orchid

soil, and really needs to have excellent drainage and plenty of air to perform well.

To transplant, remove the old bark from the orchid's roots by gently moving the roots with your fingers and cutting away the dead debris. The orchid's root is fatter than most plant roots because it has a covering to absorb and retain the orchid's water requirements.

Place the roots in the pot being careful to avoid excess damage. Ease the bark into the pot and tap the pot on a bench to settle and firm the bark around the roots. Orchids, more than any other plant family, will send root growth out of the pot. This is normal and does not mean you should transplant. Every two or three years, or when the root growth outside the pot is excessive, will be plenty of time to repot.

Now relax, you've pruned and repotted your plant into renewed beauty (and saved its life as well).

8
Health

When to call the doctor . . . I can hear you protesting on this one: "The doctor? I thought you said plants were tough, would outlive me, were simple to care for, inexpensive. . ."

They are. Plants can live a long time and with reasonable care should live from ten to fifty years or more. However, even healthy plants can get a disease, just as a healthy dog or cat can. If you want to learn about various plant diseases and how to treat them there are excellent books on the subject.

As you read, realize that there is a likelihood of your plant getting a disease, but it is just as likely that it will be treatable. A few bugs on the foliage does not mean a memorial service is in order.

First and most important—discover what's wrong with your plant as soon as possible. That's why it is a good idea to have a reference book handy. If you do suspect something is wrong you can find out what it is and do something about it. It is more difficult to eliminate an insect that's living and reproducing on a plant than one that's just landed on the leaf.

By now you've guessed that the plant doctor is not a man in a green coat who makes house calls—it's you. Start now by developing a habit of really looking at your plants when you water them.

What to Look For

1. Look for areas on a leaf or plant that have a slightly different aspect from the rest of the foliage, a slight shine or cloudy appearance. This could mean insects have arrived, most likely aphids or white flies. Many insects are so small they are impossible to see but in the process of feeding on the plant they will leave behind a slightly shiny secretion. Touch this shiny spot to see if it is sticky. If it is, you probably have some kind of insect feeding on your plant.

2. Are there brown spots on the leaves? This is not necessarily something to worry about. Brown spots could be caused by too much sun or other nondisease-related factors. How to tell? Touch the spot. If it is spongy, soggy, or damp, this indicates a rotting condition that will need attention.

3. Is there a cobweblike covering on a leaf or around a branch of your plant? This could be the work of the spider mite and the area affected will need to be treated.

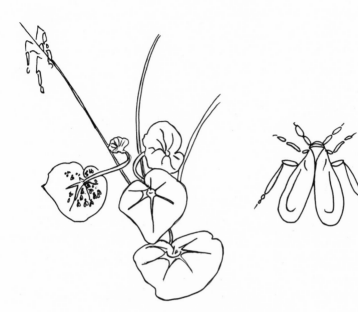

White fly on beefsteak begonia

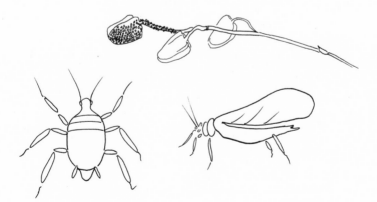

Aphid and aphid with wings on orchid bud

4. Are there small, white, cottonlike balls on the leaves or branches? Your plant may have mealybug, and treatment is called for.

Treatment

As your plant pet's doctor you will be able to treat successfully most of the ailments we've just discussed, without going to medical school.

Symptom: Sticky leaf
Treatment: The first choice is to use a chemical spray. Take the plant outside (if it is warm enough) or into a garage or basement. Give it a short spray from an aerosol insect killer. Most insect killers are all-purpose sprays designed to cover and kill a wide variety of the pests attacking your plant. I use one called House and Plant Insect spray, made by Ortho. You can also buy a concentrate and mix your own, then apply it with a sprayer, but the ready-made is more convenient.

The alternative method is to wash or spray the surface of the plant with soapy water. Put one tablespoon of Ivory detergent or any other mild detergent in a quart of water. If you have a sprayer, spray the affected area, but try to avoid getting the solution into the soil—the soap isn't good for the soil or the root system. In fact, it's not too good for the leaves, either, so don't use this treatment too often.

After spraying, leave your plant outside or wherever you have put it, until the spray dries and the odor disappears. Then bring it back in the house but keep it isolated from the rest of your plants. In four or five days spray again. This is a precautionary spray to kill eggs not annihilated by the first spray. One-time spraying is usually not enough. Those insects are tenacious. In fact, in extreme cases you may have to spray a third time in three or four days.

Symptom: Brown spots/rot condition
Treatment: Take the part of the plant that feels spongy and wet—it may also have a foul odor—and cut out the infected area. If it's the leaf, cut the whole leaf off; if it is a stem portion, then get rid of that.

If the rot has advanced down in the plant, where all growth begins, the condition may be terminal and you should consider getting rid of the plant. If you've been taking cuttings when the plant was well, you can easily grow a replacement.

Symptom: Cobweb
Treatment: Put the infected plant in the backyard, bathtub, or sink. Spray thoroughly with water to wash away the spider mite or whatever is causing the cobweb effect. Repeat every five to seven days for a couple of weeks to completely rid the plant of mites.

Symptom: Mealybug
Treatment: Catch this disease early, when there are only a few patches of mealybug on the plant, and you can get rid of them easily. Take a piece of alcohol-saturated cotton and just remove them. If the plant is heavily infested you won't be able to use the alcohol approach—it could take forever.

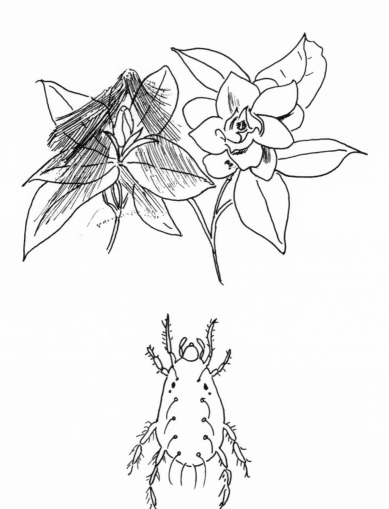

Spider mite on gardenia

Instead spray with a houseplant aerosol (two applications will usually work).

These methods should handle most of the diseases you're likely to encounter on your plants. But what if your plant gets sick and your treatment doesn't work? What do you do when your dog gets sick and the vet can't help him? You might get a second opinion. Try the plant store, or a nursery, an easier route than thumbing through a reference book trying to match up symptoms with obscure diseases and treatments.

Sad to say, of course, sometimes nothing works, and your plant doesn't get better. If we look at nature's methods we see that plants growing in the wild get diseases and they too in many cases, fail to recover. This is a way of weeding out the weaker plants and controlling the plant population. So the fact that some of your plants do not get better is not a sign that you have a brown thumb or are an unfeeling, untalented plant pet owner. The finest growers in the world lose a certain number of plants every year. They expect this, and you should realize that it does happen.

How long should you treat a sick plant? If you've been treating your pet for insect infestation or fungus for over a month and you see no improvement, then you probably had a plant that was weak in the first place, and the best thing to do is get rid of it immediately.

"But this was my plant pet," you cry. "How can you advise just letting it die?"

Mealybug on jade plant

If your dog or cat became ill beyond help you'd probably take it to the vet and have it put to sleep. And to ease your mind a little about letting go of or tossing away a diseased plant you've tried to treat, I should tell you that keeping a plant around that has some disease can be a threat to the other plants.

The thing to remember if your plant pet dies is that you can have an identical replacement. Cuttings should only be taken from well plants; therefore you should from time to time make cuttings of your prized plants as we describe later. Then you need never lose them. They will continue to reproduce themselves into many more plant pets.

9
Breeding

Rocky is such a terrific pet, strong, healthy and so cooperative that you'd like to have a few more just like him. And you can. At this point, with one plant pet thriving, you qualify as an official "green thumb." The next step is to reproduce your plant, without spending a lot of time or money. There are several ways to reproduce plants. Here are two that work for me:

Seed

The seeds available at most plant stores are usually for vegetable or annual flower plants, rather than houseplant seeds. The best sources for houseplant seeds are mail-order catalogs from plant specialty firms.

The only virtue of starting your plant from seed is (a) you can say that you did, (b) it will save you money. However, the savings are not that great compared to buying a very small plant and having a head start on the growing. The extra work and time it takes to start with seed does not justify the savings.

If you still want to start from seed, here's how to do it. Fill a two-to-three-inch pot with potting soil and then insert two or three seeds in the soil just below the surface. If you want more plants, use several pots. Starting the seeds in a pot is easier than planting them in a tray and later having to transplant them into a pot. Why not save one step and avoid disturbing the roots?

Cuttings

Propagation by cuttings is the most economical and timesaving way to reproduce plants and, despite what you may have heard or read, is a very simple procedure. In fact, you will be able to reproduce most of your houseplants by taking cuttings.

Before we start let me tell you that it takes slightly longer and is a little more difficult to reproduce a hardwood plant from a cutting. A hardwood plant has trunks and branches that are barklike (as opposed to the softer, more succulent type). This group includes the gardenia plant and the citrus plant.

HOW TO GROW FROM CUTTINGS

I'm going to describe two ways to get your cuttings started. Pick the easiest way for you.

Citrus or dwarf orange tree

The method I use. Have a cutting tray available at all times in your Living Quarters. Almost any size plastic tray will do—from four by twelve up to twelve by twenty-four inches with three- to four-inch sides. The tray should have several small holes in the bottom for drainage. The goal is to root the cuttings, not drown them. Next you'll need some rooting material. I find that vermiculite works best because it holds moisture, and garden stores usually have it on hand.

Fill your tray about two-thirds to three-fourths with the vermiculite, and water until the medium is moist. When you make a cutting insert it all the way into the vermiculite. That's all there is to it. Now just sit back and wait for the cutting to root.

Roots should take hold, strong enough for transplanting into a pot, within two weeks to two months. Swedish ivy is a fast rooter; gardenia and citrus take their time.

How can you tell if the cutting is rooting? Tug gently on the cutting—is it secure in the vermiculite? If it is, transplant at your convenience. To transplant either use an instrument (a large spoon does nicely) or just slide your finger under the bottom of the cutting and carefully lift it out, roots and all. Gently shake the plant to remove excess vermiculite. A few roots might break but there will be enough to successfully transplant your baby plant to its new pot.

The second method is slightly easier and works just as well. For some easily rooted plants (not hardwoods), take your cutting and, skipping the vermiculite/tray

Swedish ivy

step, insert the cutting directly into a pot filled with garden soil.

For example, if you want to recreate a Swedish ivy you would (1) fill a hanging pot with soil; (2) with a pencil or ice pick make holes in the soil for the number of cuttings you are going to plant; (3) put the cuttings into the holes; (4) press down lightly to secure the cuttings in the soil; (5) water. You can follow the same procedure for another plant on the list, the velvet plant. However, it will not work with the difficult-to-root plants like gardenia or citrus. You'll have to start those cuttings in a tray filled with a potting medium or root the cuttings directly into a pot filled with vermiculite, depending upon the number of cuttings.

The rooting compound, whatever brand you use, must be kept moist; moisture is extra important to baby plants—just as milk several times a day is required for a puppy or kitten. Try to keep your new plant in a slightly shaded area in your home, away from sun or strong light. The more light on the plant, the more water it will need at a time when the roots are not up to the job.

If it is an easy-to-root plant then you won't have to worry about providing a humid atmosphere. If it is difficult-to-root then those plants will need a little extra help until the baby roots can develop. Place plastic over your gardenia or citrus plant, secure the plastic around the tray, and make a few holes for air. This will create the perfect humid conditions the baby plant needs. You've just built a humidifier for a few cents.

HOW TO MAKE A CUTTING

If you read the section on pruning (pp. 62-67), you'll have no trouble. Actually, making cuttings is so easy that even if you haven't read this section you should be able to do it.

1. *Locate the top six inches of a new shoot or growth on the plant you want to reproduce.* This is where your plant's energy is focused and this part of the plant will take root quicker than cuttings from the lower part.

2. *Make the cutting just below a leaf joint on this new shoot.* Roots develop from the joints or bottom of a cutting. The more leaf joints you have in the vermiculite, the more root development.

3. *After you've made the cutting, remove the bottom leaves so that only the top two to three inches of the stem has leaves, or three to six leaves remain.* Then place this "stem" in the vermiculite to produce roots. The fewer leaves left on your cutting the less moisture the cutting will require. Without a developed root system it is difficult for your cutting to provide moisture to the rest of the "plant" in order to maintain the health of the cutting and to give it energy to support new root growth.

Why six inches and no more? This length makes it easy for the plant to sustain itself. It is also easier for a small cutting to remain upright in the vermiculite tray than a taller one.

4. *Dip the root cutting into rootone.* Rootone stimulates root growth and inhibits fungus from develop-

ing. Shake off the excess rootone by gently tapping the cutting against the side of the jar. Once you've made your cutting, try to place it in rootone as soon as possible to prevent moisture loss. The longer the cutting has to go without moisture the weaker it will get. This doesn't mean you have to drop everything and rush the cutting to the vermiculite tray; just try to get it placed within a couple of hours after being cut.

There are some plants (like the orchid) that do not lend themselves to the cutting method as a way of producing new growth. Most members of the bromeliad family will send up new growth from the base of the plant, shortly after blooming. If you leave this growth the plant will develop a cluster of bromeliad plants around the original one. These new plants may be cut off and repotted to produce a new plant. If you are going to try this, then wait until the new growth reaches about half or more of the size of the original.

The phalaenopsis orchid will not send out new growth but *occasionally* will produce a new plant from a flower spike. This flower spike will, in time, develop roots. After the roots have grown two to four inches you can cut the spike away from the parent and root this plant according to the potting instructions on orchids. But this is an exception and, in most cases, the phalaenopsis orchid will not provide cutting material.

So how do they reproduce? Either by seed or stem reproduction. This is a far more complicated technique than we need to go into here. If you are

Bromeliad or rainbow star

Lady slipper

interested in finding out more about this process and how you can learn to reproduce the phalaenopsis, it would be worthwhile to spend the time and do a little research using several of the many fine orchid books on the market. For now, if you want to own a phalaenopsis orchid, add to your collection by purchasing a small plant and then watch it develop. These orchids are not very expensive if you're buying the young plant; about $3.00 to $6.00 for a four-to-six-inch leaf spread. Once they are mature and in bloom then the price can range from $15 to $200.

The paphiopedilum or lady slipper orchid reproduces by sending out new growths from the growing medium. When there are a sufficient number of plant growths (six or more), you can split the plant to increase your collection.

Breeding or reproducing plants can be fun and rewarding. These extra plants also protect you in case your original plant dies, and of course they add to your plant pet family.

10
Playing with Your Pets

Indoors

Now, sit back and enjoy watching your pets perform. Rocky is blooming—an explosion of healthy, beautiful flowers. This is not the time to keep him in his Living Quarters. Move him to stage center where he can star for a while. If Rocky is a gardenia or citrus plant, not only will you have blooms but your room will be filled with a fragrant scent rivaling the most expensive perfume.

Move my plant out of his Living Quarters? Just when I have the light exactly right? Don't worry about your plant pet's light preference. Remember, Rocky is tough, and he'll be tolerant of his temporary home long enough for you to enjoy his blooms. In fact, many plants tend to hold their blooms longer if they're not under strong light.

You can keep your blooming plant pet in your

living space for two to three months—or longer. When Rocky stops blooming return him to Living Quarters and bring out another bloomer. That way you can have a parade of flowers right where you can enjoy them.

Or, since Rocky looks great on your glass corner table, can you keep him there permanently? Even if that corner is dimly lit? Yes you can, though you may want to consider adding one or two flood or spotlights. The visual effect of a well-placed spotlight on a blooming plant is spectacular, and spots especially designed for plants will provide your plant with a balanced color spectrum. There are special small fixtures that are easy to install and that will fit into any decor.

You need to remember: A spot or floodlight is fine for keeping most plants healthy, but it may be inadequate for a plant that needs a large, daily dose of light to begin to bloom. Give your plant a year to bloom in your living room. If no blooms come after that your plant needs additional, intense light. Move Rocky to a window where he will get sun, or move him to his Living Quarters and set up more light, or, during the summer move him outdoors. Don't forget to provide some shade; most plants can't take the summer sun full force every day.

Outdoors

Outside there are two options:

1. If you have a yard and a tree, try hanging your plants from hooks in the trees. The hooks, which

Flame violet or starlight

you can get from a garden shop or direct-mail cata-
log, anchor onto the side of the plant's pot and then
can be attached to the tree. A tree covered with
hanging blooming plants is a spectacular sight.
You're also doing your plant a favor by getting it up
and away from kids, dogs, and cats, who occasionally
like to take a nibble of a plant leaf.

Checking your plant's soil for wet or dry conditions is a snap when the plant is hanging—use the
methods outlined in Chapter 6.

No tree? Then, for the summer, put your plants in
the garden by sinking the pot into the soil. But *don't*
take the plant out of the pot. If you do, you'll find
that the roots, ecstatic about being in the wide world
of dirt, will quickly outgrow the pot. Then you'll
have to cut them back when you bring the plant back
in the house.

Cutting back in itself is not harmful but you're
already asking the plant to make an adjustment
switching from outdoors to indoors, and that's
enough.

If you do put Rocky in the ground, leave the top
half inch of the pot above the surface of the ground.
This will help prevent the roots from growing over
the top of the pot into the surrounding soil. My final
suggestion is that you place some kind of a mulch,
such as wood chips over the pot in order to help
keep moisture in the pot during the summer. There
is a tendency for the soil in the pot to dry out slightly
faster than the soil around it, especially if the pot is
plastic.

In the fall you can dig up the pot or lift it down

from its tree to bring your plant indoors again. Sometimes a plant returning indoors will react to the change by losing some leaves. This is normal and nothing to worry about. The leaf loss will usually be at the lower bottom of the plant or branches. If the new or top growth is browning and dropping then that means trouble. Check for disease and soil condition.

Several plant varieties do not want to spend their summer vacation outside—they really can't take the sun, even in the shade. Check the list in the appendix for the sunny outdoor type. They include: the gardenia, citrus plants, hibiscus, and jade plant. The jade plant loves sun and needs it for blooms.

Moving into the Big Time

As you begin to feel comfortable with your plant pets you'll probably want to know more about plants in general. Here are a few places to start:

Plant shop or local nursery. Good places to observe different plant varieties. They will also give you a chance to get answers to some of your plant pet questions.

Flower shows. Most communities have some kind of flower show. This is an excellent opportunity to see plant varieties at their Sunday best. You will also be able to talk to the experts, purchase plants and supplies not available locally. People associated with the flower industry are friendly and usually eager to

Jade plant

help you. Don't be shy about asking questions about the plants you own or the ones in the show.

Botanical gardens. Here is where you can see magnificent displays of plants, including houseplants, from all over the world, without traveling. When you do travel you'll find it worthwhile to visit the botanical gardens in the city you're visiting. If you're there at the right time you may be able to attend their flower show as well.

Garden clubs. This is where you not only learn more about your plant pets but you have an opportunity to meet other people who are interested in them as well. Trade and exchange plants here; listen to speakers and when you're ready, display Rocky at the club's flower show.

Giving Your Pets Away

And now a word for those of you who have moved into the big time and no longer have space in your plant Living Quarters and even in the rest of your house for all the pets you've taken under your wing: What better gift can you offer a friend who's ill or just depressed than a blooming plant pet? The friend can have a beautiful companion and the pet can have a dose of special attention. Your pets can also be Christmas gifts—dress up Rocky's children in big red bows and give them to everyone on your list. You might want to tie on a tag telling the new owner something about their pet. One friend I know even sent Christmas cards with pictures of her plants

Fig plant

and a message that read "Stop by and pick me up." You can even bring a plant along to your next dinner party for the host and hostess instead of a bottle of wine. The possibilities are endless.

For all of you who have tried and not succeeded with plants over the years, I urge you to try again. Now you know it's *not* hard to establish a routine which will allow you and your plants to have a flourishing relationship.

I Want You to Remember:

Worry less—use common sense.
Have Living Quarters for your plant pets.
Don't overwater.
Prune—with confidence.

You don't need a green thumb to raise healthy, beautiful pets, just an evergreen attitude that will allow you to disregard plant myths and your own fears, and find out what the plants have known all along—they're the easiest pets to own.

APPENDIX I

Suggested Plant Pets for the New Pet Owner

Here's a list of plants from different plant families. Their characteristics vary and their requirements do too. They range from easy-to-grow to "exotic" families, like orchids. But don't let the exotic ones scare you—they require only slightly more attention than the easy-to-grow. This list includes plant pets for people who feel they can't grow anything, as well as plant pets that are slightly different from the run-of-the-mill variety for you adventurers.

1. *Swedish Ivy*

Anybody can handle this nifty little plant. Great in a hanging pot, it does well in ordinary pots too. The leaves are heavy-textured and round, about the size of a half-dollar to a silver dollar. If you grow it in the house without much light, the leaves will be dark green. In a brighter light, like early morning or afternoon sun, they turn a paler shade of green.

Grow it in some sun or very bright light and it will produce small clusters of white flowers. Size is no problem, just cut back or prune this rapidly spreading plant. The cut-back portions can easily be rooted to make additional plants.

2. *Spider Plant*

You can grow the spider plant anywhere in the house. It is practically indestructible, with a lot of character, takes neglect beautifully, and on top of all that it is a very interesting plant.

It has long, thin leaves that grow out from the center cluster and range anywhere from twelve to eighteen inches long; the leaves are usually green-and-white striped, but it is also available in solid green.

This plant has a personality and does something really charming—it sends out one-and-a-half to two-feet spikes or stems which produce a small, white flower. After the flower drops off a new plant will develop off the end of the spike. Each one will produce its own long, thin, green leaves and send out a root structure. You can imagine the interesting affect the spider plant is capable of producing when ten to twenty-five small plants are cascading off these spikes. If left uncut, the new spikes send out more spikes which will create a third tier of new plants.

To control this profusion of tiers you need to regulate the spider plant's light; the more bright light or sun, the more spikes. After some root structure has developed on your new plants you can cut and repot them right into the soil of the original plant or into new pots to make additional plants.

3. *Hoya or Wax Plant*

The wax plant is named for its flowers. They are about the size of a pea and clustered together in a half-sphere shape. The individual flowers are very heavy textured and waxlike in appearance. The blooms seem almost unreal. In addition to this exotic flower the wax plant boasts very attractive foliage.

You'll have many varieties of wax plant to choose from, some with solid green leaves, others with variegated green, and one that has a curly green leaf, nicknamed the "hindu rope plant." It makes an excellent candidate for a hanging pot as the leaves protrude from a long stem that grows downward and remains fairly tight and slow growing.

Your wax plant pet is not difficult to grow if you remember it likes to dry out between waterings. If you want blooms just see that it gets bright light or early morning or afternoon sun. Even if you are not able to provide sun, the foliage is reason enough to grow this charming plant.

Maintenance is a snap; just cut back to control the growth. Again, like the spider plant, the cuttings can easily be rooted back in the original pot or placed in a separate pot to produce another wax plant. For beauty and dramatic effect, I would put it in a hanging pot but it does very nicely as a potted plant, too.

4. *Espicia or Starlight*

I have named this plant the "starlight" because of its striking white trumpet-shaped flower fringed around the small opening. The dime-sized leaves are green and fuzzy-textured. Starlight grows very compactly and is excellent for hanging pots as it will grow downward in a tight, ball-like form. It also does well in a pot.

The mature plant looks like a long ball or cone and is very attractive for its foliage alone. If you want to achieve a large quantity of the white starlight flowers, which are spectacular against the green growth, only a little bright light or sun is required. Your starlight plant pet will need slightly warmer conditions than the plants listed earlier, some extra humidity, and a little more bright light. Given these requirements you will not find it difficult to grow and you will be rewarded with a profusion of lovely blooms for very little effort.

5. *Beefsteak Begonia*

Sounds hardy, doesn't it? And it is. This will make an excellent plant pet. It has large shiny green flat leaves about the size of a tomato. The underside of the leaf has a reddish cast to it. This is another compact growing plant with a vast amount of leaves. It will produce flowers on spikes about one foot tall with a cluster of light, or pinkish, small flowers at the top.

Beefsteak is very easy to grow and will tolerate almost any condition in your house. By now you know that some light is required to produce blooms and the beefsteak begonia is no exception. But again, it is attractive for its foliage alone if getting sunlight to it is too much trouble. It will bloom very nicely, though, under a fluorescent light.

6. *Jade Plant*

This is an attractive and almost indestructible plant and will make an outstanding pet. The jade plant is a very slow-growing plant, with almost a bonzai character. Because it is grown primarily for its succulent light green foliage on a very thick, solid trunk and branches, most people are unaware that the jade plant blooms. Most jade plants are brought into the house and there they stay in insufficient light, looking quite beautiful but with no blooms. If you're interested in producing the very small, star-light white flowers on a tight cluster (with a very nice aroma) just put your jade plant out during the long, sunny summer days. Don't expect blooms from a baby jade. Wait until your plant is mature and grows to a good size, about twelve inches or more.

The jade plant in bloom will be covered with flowers for two to three weeks. If you opt for no blooms you can still experiment with the color of the foliage—dark green in a dark corner, light green in direct sun.

7. *Purple Velvet Plant*

As you might conclude from the dramatic name, this plant is somewhat unusual. It is listed here for those of you who want to try something different but not impossible. Velvet is very easy to grow and will do well under most conditions.

The foliage is velvetlike with purple veins; the underside has almost a reddish tint and the contrast between the two sides is quite striking. Put this one in an ordinary pot or a hanging pot. It tends to grow upright but if it gets long enough it will hang over and push down toward the floor.

To keep your purple velvet compact, just prune. You'll be rewarded with greater branching and a nice full look. There are flowers, small and orange, which last only a few days but are a pretty contrast to the foliage. I know you know by now how to produce blooms—just provide some light, natural or fluorescent.

You can have many purple velvet plants for the price of one if you plant your cuttings.

8. *Christmas Cactus*

This may be a familiar, old standby but it is a rewarding plant pet to own. In fact, there are many varieties in the cactus family and you may want to experiment with a few. They do great if you keep them on the dry side.

This cactus has an interesting appearance, foliage that continues to grow out in a cactuslike fashion. For greater branching form, just cut back. However, if you like the way it is growing (it grows relatively slowly), forget about pruning.

At Christmastime (surprise) the Christmas cactus will produce a striking, red flower. There is another cactus called the Thanksgiving cactus; can you guess when it blooms?

You really don't have to do much for the Christmas cactus. Just provide a windowsill where it can cool off every night and some light during the day.

9. *Gardenia or "Queen Bee"*

I am going to spend a little more time telling you about the gardenia because it is a magnificent plant, what I call the "queen bee" of plants. It has a dramatic, glossy white, heavy-textured flower about four to five inches across which will provide a rich, heady scent that will fill your rooms better than the most expensive perfumes.

But . . .

Of all the plants I have listed, the gardenia is the most difficult to grow. Now, don't panic. I said difficult, not impossible. If you want to have success as a gardenia plant pet owner you'll need to provide the queen bee with the following in this order of priority:

1. Plenty of water
2. Some sun
3. An acid soil condition

Despite what some plant books say about the gardenia wanting to dry out between waterings, I have found that this is one plant you can't water too much. You can mist your plant but you don't have to—just make sure its soil is always moist.

Provide your plant with a good-sized pot, filled with potting soil to which you can add some humus, and place the pot in a saucer. The saucer will allow you to water the gardenia until the soil is saturated. Check the saucer—if there is water in it you know the soil is still moist; if not, then it's time to water again. During hot, dry days you may have to water daily; during a cooler period every two to three or three to four days. *Tip:* Frequent watering will prevent the queen bee's leaves from yellowing or the buds from dropping off.

There is no avoiding this requirement: If you want a blooming gardenia you will have to make sure your plant gets a good morning or afternoon sun. You can use bright or fluorescent lights but the blooms will not be as good. An alternative is to take the gardenia outdoors in the summer.

The last item, acid soil, is easy to achieve if your water contains acid; if not, just add peat moss—this will increase the acidity. If you have high-alkaline water add cottonseed mill or one of the many acid fertilizers.

This plant grows upright and will send out branches which can get quite long. Yearly pruning is called for to shape and keep your plant compact. If the pruning is done right after the flowering season there will be plenty of time for the plant to produce new growth and be ready to bloom again the following spring.

10. *Hibiscus*

I have nicknamed this plant the "elegant hummingbird." The stem protruding from its flower center reminds me of the hummingbird's beak and its large flower petals resemble the hummingbird's constantly moving wings.

The hibiscus grows into a very large shrub with handsome green foliage and showy, wide, colorful flowers. The flowers are around four to seven or eight inches wide! Like the "now you see him now you don't" hummingbird, the hibiscus's flowers do a disappearing act after only a few days. Fortunately, the bush produces a nice quantity of flowers over a two-to-six month period.

This plant is easy to grow if you provide it with sufficient light, and it will tolerate most conditions, including a very dry climate. As you probably have already guessed, hibiscus needs sun in order to produce sufficient blooming. Fluorescent lights will work if the plant is close to the light source.

To keep your plant pet looking sharp you'll need to prune annually—this is a big plant. If it's done in late summer, like the gardenia it will regain its growth and bloom again the following summer.

11. *Citrus Plant*

This family includes orange, dwarf orange, lemon, kumquat, and others. My choice is the dwarf orange which I call JO or junior orange. JO is easy to grow and will stay more compact in its growing habit than the rest of the citrus family. It has an attractive green leaf slightly smaller than the larger citrus plants and a nice branching form.

JO is a triple-threat plant—lovely flowers, delicious scent, and those wonderful, small, brightly colored oranges. To produce the flowering and the oranges JO will need slightly brighter light than most plants. You can provide this by putting your plant in the garden during the summer for the early morning or late afternoon sunlight—or grow it in a sunny window or on a porch. If you keep the fluorescent light close enough (twenty to thirty inches) it will bloom under it as well.

12. *Bromeliad Tricolor*

The bromeliad, also known as the rainbow star, has an interesting history. About twenty years ago it could be found in practically every home in America, but today it is rarely seen. Why? For the same reason that a particular animal is high on the popularity list and then is replaced by a different breed. Styles and fads come and go in the plant pet world too.

However, the same qualities that made it a favorite years ago can be enjoyed by you today. The rainbow star has everything one could want in a houseplant. It will tolerate almost any living conditions, is suited to dry climates, is very hardy, is disease-free, and does not require much pruning. Plus—it has beautiful foliage which varies in color depending upon the amount of light you provide.

This plant even comes with its own watering cup. The foliage grows from a center base and forms a cup where water is stored. Just keep the cup full and the plant will absorb what it needs. Once-a-week watering is sufficient because this plant pet likes to dry out.

The leaves of the rainbow star are eight inches to a foot long and are green-and-white striped. When it gets sufficient light, pink and red stripes appear and give the plant its rainbow quality. The leaves will branch out from the cup to form the star. Rainbow star will be in full color for many months when natural or fluorescent light is provided. New plants shoot up from the base and these plants can be grown in the same container, giving the plant a full effect, or they can be cut off and transplanted.

Bromeliads are not as available in the flower shops as they should be, but mail-order houses handle them. This family is large and there are many bromeliads, all of which are hardy and offer a range of color foliage and flower spikes, depending upon the variety. It is really an excellent plant.

13. *Paphiopedilum or Lady Slipper Orchid*

We can call this plant pet "paph" for short but I'd better identify it further or you won't be impressed with something called paph. This plant is a member of the largest plant family (35,000 species) in the world—the orchid family.

Before you start saying, "Oh, I couldn't possibly grow an orchid. Let's move on to the next plant," did you know that orchids grow on every continent in the world in varied environments for different species? Now I know you will not be able to provide the growing requirements for all 35,000 species but out of this vast family there are many that will flourish for you as a houseplant pet.

First, to have success as an orchid owner you have to forget everything you've ever heard about them. That they are delicate, impossible to grow, and very expensive. I think the orchid myth continues to grow because the only time we ever come in contact with one is in the form of an expensive corsage—a corsage that must be rushed to the refrigerator if it is going to survive long enough to make the event for which it was purchased. We certainly never saw people growing orchids the way they did ivy, violets, and geraniums. Therefore the orchid, beautiful and expensive, must be as fragile as a champagne bubble.

Well, this is not true. You can grow orchids, such as the paph, under normal house conditions and produce beautiful flowers. The paph is a bit unusual because in addition to having a beautiful flower, its foliage is interesting as well. Most orchid plants are really not that attractive, the flower is what counts. The leaves of the paph protrude from a center core running from six to nine inches in length and are various shades of mottled green.

Additional plants will continue to grow from the center core forming a group of plants all in the same pot with a mass of attractive foliage. Each plant can produce an orchid flower that will last for a month or more. The flowers are truly spectacular—you'll have to grow one to find out. The illustration will give you some idea of the character of this unique flower—green stripes on a white background.

You can grow paph under a fluorescent light or in a windowsill exposure where it will get bright light or early morning/late afternoon sun. If light is not adequate the plant will fail to bloom each year as it normally does. Remember, light requirements are not complicated or even great, it can still bloom in an area where there is no sun at all but just brief bright light.

14. *Phalaenopsis or Moth Orchid*

As you can see, I have a slight bias toward the orchid family. The moth orchid is probably my favorite plant variety; the only one running close to it is the gardenia. But, and I bet you'll be surprised at this, the moth orchid is a lot easier to grow than the gardenia.

The moth orchid is a small plant, yet a mature phalaenopsis can have anywhere from ten to even fifty blooms on a single plant, each bloom being from two to up to five inches wide and round in shape with a range of colors—white, pink, yellow, stripes. As if that isn't enough from one little plant, each flower will last anywhere from two to three months—the overall effect: a plant blooming for up to almost half the year. The flowers extend from a long spike running from a foot to two feet in height which gracefully arcs, forming a magnificent display of color.

The solid green foliage is six to fifteen inches long coming out of a center core. The foliage, like most orchid plants, is not strikingly beautiful, but certainly not unattractive.

As far as lighting goes, you can relax. It will do beautifully under fluorescent light and will also grow in any area in your house with bright light. It does not need sun—in fact too much sun will burn the leaves. Early morning sun or late afternoon is fine and will insure good-size blooms.

The moth orchid does like to be watered thoroughly once every three to four days if the conditions are dry, or once every week if it is humid. So, this is the hard part, I can hear you saying. Not so. If you have placed your orchid in a place primarily for decoration and it is inconvenient to water it there, just pick it up and place it under the faucet in your sink or tub, let the water run through it for a minute. Then put it back in its showplace.

This orchid does prefer to grow on a tree bark or tree fern, items that simulate its natural situation. You can find bark and fern in any of the orchid supply houses. These supply houses are very dependable and can ship phalaenopsis or other orchids in perfect condition.

I recommend that you explore the magic and beauty of the moth orchid.

There is a final group of hardy foliage plants that will grow under almost any conditions. They are attractive green-leafed plants that can add life and color to all parts of your house. They will survive well with very little light and can take neglect with great ease.

15. *Corn Plant*

This is a member of the dracaena family, which can grow to be quite tall and stunning. There are quite a few varieties in this family, all of which grow to be fairly large sized, have very attractive foliage, a lot of which is variegated, adding to the pleasant effect. Most of the plants in this family are almost indestructible and get along with very little light. They prefer some humidity but respond well to house temperatures and are able to take dry conditions. Another good member of this group is the dragon tree, also known by the family name of dracaena.

16. *Fig Plant*

The Latin name is ficus and it is a very large family comprising almost a thousand species. One of the more common is the weeping fig, which has a very attractive appearance because of its drooping branches. The fig plant can grow to be very large and is therefore excellent for adding green touches to your home. It will do well at house temperatures. It prefers a slight amount of light, but not sun. It does better if not moved too much because it does have difficulty in adjusting to a new location. If moved frequently it will lose some of its leaves but it will recover in time. The soil should be kept somewhat on the moist side, but on the whole this is a tolerant group of plants.

17. *Radiator Plant or Peperomia*

This again is a large family with well over a thousand species. It is a smaller growing plant with very decorative foliage. It does like some light which you can achieve by placing it near a window, but it should be kept out of direct sunlight. House temperatures are perfect and it will survive very well in the normal humidity of your home. It prefers to dry out between waterings. You will generally find forms of this plant in most garden or nursery outlets and you should select your plants on the basis of how the foliage appeals to you.

APPENDIX II

Latin Name	Family Name	Plant's Personality	Nickname
HANGING POTS			
Hoya	Asclepiadaceae	Flowers jewellike and look almost unreal	Wax plant
Episcia dianthiflora	Gesneriaceae	Small leaves, compact growing, with starlike flowers	Flame violet or starlight
Chlorophytum	Liliaceae	Long, thin, spidery leaves sending out long shoots	Spider plant
Plectranthus	Labiatae	Dense, creeping, with small, leathery, waxy, round leaves	Swedish ivy
SMALL POT PLANTS			
Begonia erythrophylla	Begoniaceae	Creeping, leathery, glossy, large, round leaves (red underneath)	Beefsteak
Crassula arborescens	Crassulaceae	Thick, fleshy, rounded upper surface leaves, jade-green color	Jade plant
Gynura	Compositae	Fleshy leaves, velvetlike with purple veins	Velvet plant
Zygocactus	Cactaceae	Produces abundance of striking red blooms at Christmastime	Christmas cactus

LARGE POT PLANTS			
Gardenia	Rubiaceae	Large (4"–5") white flowers, extremely fragrant, majestic in appearance	Queen bee or opera gardenia
Hibiscus	Maluaceae	Large (4"–6") many-colored flowers with long center sepal	Elegant Hummingbird or Chinese Rose
Citrus taitensis	Rutaceae	Attractive foliage with dwarf oranges	Orangey
EXOTIC PLANTS			
Cryptanthus bromelioides tricolor	Bromeliaceae	Thick, colorful foliage growing from center crown like a star	Rainbow star
Paphiopedilum	Orchidaceae	Very showy, multicolored, large flower	Lady slipper
Phalaenopsis	Orchidaceae	Long spike of flat flowers looking like moth with wings spread	Moth orchid
FOLIAGE PLANTS			
Dracaena fragrans	Liliaceae	Long, broad, green leaves with yellowish stripe growing off large trunk	Corn plant
Ficus benjamina	Moraceae	Shiny, small green leaves on long weeping branches	Weeping fig
Peperomia argyreia	Piperaceae	Roundish, shiny, light-green leaves with dark-green pattern	Radiator plant

APPENDIX III

Plants	Growing Habits	Length of Blooming	Number of Blooms	Foliage
HANGING POTS				
Wax plant	Slow growing long vines that wrap around supports or interweave with other vines	1-2 months with each bloom lasting 2-3 weeks	5-20 clusters of many small flowers	Heavy texture with shiny leaves
Flame violet or starlight	Very compact growing with runners winding together	1-2 months with each bloom 2-5 days	20-50	Small, round leaves with fuzzy surface
Spider	Many thin leaves growing from center cone	1-2 weeks	Cluster of very small flowers	Long glossy, very thin leaves
Swedish ivy	Dense, creeping foliage	1-2 weeks	Many small blooms on each cluster	Leathery, waxy leaves, almost round
SMALL POT PLANTS				
Beefsteak	Creeping, low growing and compact	2-3 weeks for bloom	5-10 very small flowers on spike; produces many spikes	Large, round glossy leaves
Jade plant	Compact treelike plant	2-3 weeks	Cluster of small white flowers	Thick, fleshy leaves
Velvet plant	Vinelike, needs pruning	4-7 days	Small orange-colored flowers	Velvety leaves with purple coloring
Christmas cactus	Compact, slow growing	3-5 days	Single striking orange flowers	Thick leathery leaves

LARGE POT PLANTS				
Opera gardenia	Compact plant or bush if pruned	7-10 days each bloom	5-10 small plant; 25-50 large plant	Shiny, green leaves
Chinese rose (hibiscus)	Fast growing, large shrub needs to be pruned	2-3 days each bloom but plant in bloom for months	25-50 on large plant over blooming period	Green, ragged edge leaves
Citrus	Compact plant shaped like large orange tree	3-4 days with fragrance	10-25 during blooming period	Attractive, small green leaves
FOLIAGE PLANTS				
Corn plant	Tall plant, leaves from tall trunk	None		Long, broad, green leaves
Weeping fig	Large plant, will need pruning	None		Many, smallish green leaves on weeping branches
Radiator plant	Compact, small plant	Not of interest		Light green, roundish leaves, dark green pattern
EXOTIC PLANTS				
Rainbow star (bromeliad)	Small plant with long, thick leaves	Not of interest		Long, shiny colorful leaves
Lady slipper	Compact, low-growing plant	3-4 weeks each bloom	1-5 blooms depending upon size of plant	Long (6"-9") leaves
Moth orchid	Compact, low-growing plant	2-3 months each bloom	5-25 on long spikes	Long (6"-12") fleshy leaves

APPENDIX IV

Plant	Temperature	Humidity	Soil	Light	Watering
HANGING POTS					
Wax plant	Warm	Moderate	Garden soil	Bright	Dry out
Flame violet or starlight	Warm	High	Rich in organic matter	Bright	Moist
Spider plant	Intermediate	Moderate	Garden soil	Bright	Moist
Swedish ivy	Warm	Tolerates dry conditions	Garden soil	Bright	Moist
SMALL POT PLANTS					
Beefsteak begonia	Warm	Moderate	Rich in organic matter	Bright	Moist
Jade plant	Intermediate	Moderate	Garden soil	Sun	Dry out
Velvet plant	Warm	Moderate	Garden soil	Bright	Moist
Christmas cactus	Warm	Moderate	Rich in organic matter	Bright	Moist

	Temperature	Humidity	Soil	Light	Water
LARGE POT PLANTS					
Opera gardenia or queen bee	Warm	Moderate	Rich in organic matter	Sun	Very moist
Hibiscus	Warm	Moderate	Garden soil	Sun	Moist
Citrus	Intermediate	Moderate	Garden soil	Sun	Dry out
FOLIAGE PLANTS					
Corn plant	Warm	Moderate	Garden soil	Bright	Moist
Weeping fig	Warm	Moderate	Garden soil	Bright	Moist
Radiator plant	Warm	High	Rich in organic matter	Bright	Dry out
EXOTIC PLANTS					
Rainbow star (bromeliad)	Warm	Tolerates dry conditions	Rich in organic matter	Bright	Dry out
Lady slipper (paphiopedilum)	Warm	High	Rich in organic material or fern fiber	Shady	Moist
Moth Orchid	Warm	High	Fir bark or fern fiber	Shady	Moist